FORGOTTEN

ELLIS ISLAND

The Extraordinary Story of America's Immigrant Hospital

LORIE CONWAY

CONTEMPORARY PHOTOGRAPHS BY CHRIS BARNES

 Smithsonian Books

Collins

An Imprint of HarperCollinsPublishers

This book is lovingly dedicated to my son, Max George,
whose great-grandfather Edward Conway immigrated to
America in 1900 at the age of 18. Arriving at Ellis Island
from Ballina, Ireland, he had two dollars in his pocket and
listed his occupation as "laborer." By 1915, he was already
living the American dream—he had a family, owned a
home, and in one photo, a derby hat sits jauntily on his
head, his Irish eyes smiling as if he had not a care in the
world. May my son Max fulfill his own dream,
wherever that may lead him.

HarperCollins books may be purchased for educational, business, or sales promotional use. For information, please write: Special Markets Department, HarperCollins Publishers, 10 East 53rd Street, New York, NY 10022.

First Smithsonian Books edition published 2007.

Designed by JUDITH STAGNITTO ABBATE / ABBATE DESIGN
Contemporary photos can be found at CHRISTOPHERBARNES.COM.

The Library of Congress Cataloging in Publication Data has been applied for.

ISBN: 978-0-06-124196-3
ISBN-10: 0-06-124196-2

07 08 09 10 11 TOP 10 9 8 7 6 5 4 3 2 1

CONTENTS

FOREWORD

THE FORGOTTEN STORY OF THE IMMIGRANT HOSPITAL ON ELLIS ISLAND HAS BEEN A PART OF MY LIFE SINCE 1998. A FRIEND REMARKED: "IT'S AS IF SOMEONE TAPPED YOU ON

the shoulder and said, 'Your mission is to tell this story.'"

My story began when I called Frank Mills, deputy superintendent at the site of the Statue of Liberty and Ellis Island, asking about the possibility of creating a documentary film on the history of the massive, abandoned hospital complex. My interest had been kindled by a *New York Times Magazine* article that described Ellis Island as being "as close to a national shrine as we have in America" while suggesting at the same time that a major part of its history—the hospital story—had not been told. Speaking a few days later with a National Park Service representative, I learned that no book or film had been

produced about the hospital despite its intriguing history. In its day, the hospital was one of the world's great and most modern. Yet, within five decades after being built, it was virtually abandoned.

Starting in 1999, the National Park Service gave my production company exclusive access for a year to film the hospital buildings. Today, they are undergoing restoration and will eventually include a public health museum and an immigration institute. When we filmed them, however, the buildings were laced with poison ivy, loose asbestos, and flaking lead paint. A tree had taken root in the cracked linoleum floor outside one of the operating rooms. In rain and snow, at dawn and at dusk, from the ground and from helicopter, we captured images of the hospital—everything from the psychopathic hospital and autopsy amphitheater to the contagious disease hospital and diagnostic laboratory. As we filmed, we thought about the thousands of immigrant patients who had peered through the windows at the Statue of Liberty as they lay in the white iron beds lining the wards. The filming of two former patients at the hospital location brought the institution even further to life. As one of them walked through the hospital, where he had been admitted as a five-year-old boy newly arrived from France, he recalled the anxiety he felt as his mother was told she could not remain with him.

The idea of being the first to research this forgotten chapter of Ellis Island's history has carried me through a long and sometimes frustrating effort. My search took me through dusty files at the National Archives, the New York Public Library, the Public Health Archives, Ellis Island Library, Widener Library at Harvard, and other institutions. As it happens, there is no central repository of the hospital's records, despite tantalizing hints that they might be found in federal archives in Washington

or Louisiana or Colorado. Nevertheless, the hospital's story slowly came together piece by piece. Paging through the personal scrapbooks of William Williams, a two-term Ellis Island commissioner, I discovered a man ambivalent about immigration but determined to build a hospital for immigrants and convinced that the patients should be treated with "kindness and consideration." A month before this manuscript went to the publisher, the family of Ormond McDermott, a 19-year-old who died in the hospital of scarlet fever, was located in Sydney, Australia. His medical record was one of the few to survive after the hospital was abandoned. Five years after discovering Ormond's file, I finally had a face to attach to the medical notes that charted his last days alive.

While researching the hospital's history, I discovered that today's immigration controversies are not markedly different from those of a century ago. The faces of today's newcomers differ, but the arguments for and against their entry have changed little from those aired in the early 1900s. Even the themes and images of the editorial cartoons of that earlier era resemble those in today's periodicals. Immigration is a timeless American story, and I consider myself fortunate to be able to tell a part of it.

The main reason for telling the hospital's story, however, is for its merit as a publicly funded institution. During the hospital's busiest years, from 1902–1930, immigrants who arrived in America with diseases were treated with suspicion but also with kindness and with care. The doctors of the U.S. Public Health Service had a twofold mission—to heal the sick but also to protect the nation from the diseases the immigrants carried. The hospital was not a perfect place. An unknown number of new arrivals were deported for medical diagnoses based more on how "true" Americans were supposed to look and act than on the threat they posed to the public health. But a much larger number of immigrants—tens of thousands—were restored to health in the hospital and granted entry after having initially been disqualified for medical reasons. There were also fortunate accidents of birth—350 immigrant babies were born at the hospital, automatically becoming U.S. citizens.

These and other stories make up the forgotten history of the Ellis Island Hospital. It is a history lost to all but the generation that lived it. This book seeks to change that reality.

FORGOTTEN

ELLIS ISLAND

CHAPTER I

CONSTRUCTING THE IMMIGRANT HOSPITAL

"IT WAS A GENERAL HOSPITAL OF ALL NATIONS."

"No man would invite a person afflicted with a contagious disease beneath his roof, to mingle with members of his own family. Rather would he shield his family from contact with disease; and as the nation is but a larger family every citizen should do his part, use his influence, to safeguard the homes of the poor of the United States against disease from abroad."[1]

TERRENCE POWDERLY,
Commissioner General of Immigration, 1902

As THE STEAMSHIP *MORAVIA* HEADED INTO NEW YORK HARBOR ON AUGUST 30, 1892, THE MARINE HOSPITAL SERVICE (MHS) DOCTORS ON ELLIS ISLAND BRACED FOR THE WORST.

The cholera epidemic then ravaging Asia and Europe—150,000 dead in Russia alone—had infected the ship's passengers. Twenty-four had been stricken with the illness, and 22 of them had died—all but two of the dead were children under the age of 10. Surviving passengers had panicked, throwing the dead overboard "as if they were dead birds or garbage."[2]

Three times previously in the 19th century, the United States had suffered a devastating cholera outbreak, each originating abroad. Would the *Moravia*'s arrival mark the start of the fourth?

Opened as a port of entry only eight months earlier, Ellis Island was poorly equipped to handle the threat. Its two-story wooden dispensary had neither the staff nor the laboratory to contain a disease as deadly as cholera. Believing he had no other choice, Dr. W. T. Jenkins, the Port of New York's health officer, ordered the *Moravia* to anchor offshore until the outbreak was contained. Five days later, two more "death ships," the *Rugia* and *Normannia*, steamed into New York Harbor, and they, too, were ordered to anchor offshore. Dr. Jenkins warned that anyone—passenger or crew member—who tried to leave the quarantined ships would be shot. More than a thousand passengers were stranded on the ships, and they begged to be let off, terrified that sick passengers would soon infect them. Their plea was denied. Over the next several days, additional cases broke out, killing most of the infected passengers within a day. Not until nearly three weeks had passed were the healthy passengers finally allowed to disembark.[3]

Was the inadequacy of the medical facility at Ellis Island partly to blame for the additional deaths?[4] Health authorities could not easily dismiss the possibility. The arriving passengers might all have lived had they been immediately removed from the ships and quarantined at a safe medical facility.

The issue of how to protect the health of both the nation and the immigrant would hover over Ellis Island for the next decade. Its existing medical facility was not equipped to handle anything but routine illness. When the wooden infirmary caught fire and burned to the ground in 1897, the problem became dire. A makeshift hospital was established in an old house on Ellis Island, but it was small and poorly appointed. Passengers with infectious diseases such as measles and diphtheria

were shuttled to neighboring hospitals, which increasingly refused to take them. Although New York's indigent hospital, Bellevue, remained open to immigrants for several years to come, even it eventually stopped taking such patients. The city's health commissioner, Ernst Lederle, told reporters: "The patients from Ellis Island should not be brought into the city limits at all. They are a source of infection from the time they leave the island until they reach the foot of East 16th Street. Besides, they have to be placed in wards where they subject other patients to the danger of mixed infection."[5]

Ironically, fears of immigrant-borne disease were mounting at a time when medical breakthroughs raised hopes that many illnesses could be corralled. The science of medicine was being redefined by the work of Joseph Lister, Louis Pasteur, and Robert Koch. They had identified bacilli responsible for several killer diseases, and experimental vaccines were being developed.

Immigrants on board a steamship en route to Ellis Island.
"Our rules, our laws in regard to the admission of immigrants are much more rigid than they were a century ago, and Mr. William Williams, the new commissioner of immigration at Ellis Island, is watching the gate very closely." AMERICAN BOY, 1902.

Nevertheless, old ideas about disease had a powerful hold on the general public and fed concerns about immigrants, particularly the huge wave of new entrants from southern and eastern Europe. These arrivals were visibly poorer and less well-kempt than the earlier arrivals from northern Europe and carried strange diseases like favus and trachoma. New Hampshire senator William Chandler said: "No one has suggested a race distinction. We are confronted with the fact, however, that the poorest immigrants do come from certain races."[6] *The New York Times* in an editorial was more direct: "We do not want and we ought to refuse to land all or any of these unclean Italians or Russian Hebrews. We have enough dirt, misery, crime, sickness, and death of our own without permitting any more to be thrust upon us."[7] Alabama senator J. Thomas Heflin, a rabid nativist, called these immigrants "the greatest evil that has confronted us in a century."[8]

Hostility toward the new arrivals was lessened by a hard fact: the United States needed them. America's Industrial Revolution had started later than Europe's but was now overtaking it. Labor was in short supply. "Industry is developing,

workers are in demand," wrote one observer. "Without them the country cannot maintain its present pace."[9]

In his first State of the Union message in 1901, President Theodore Roosevelt proposed a change in immigration policy that would thrust the medical facility at Ellis Island into national prominence. Roosevelt said that America should open its gates to the able-bodied while barring entry to the weak and the infirm. "We can not have too much immigration of the right kind," said Roosevelt, "and we should have none of the wrong kind." In order to keep out what he called "undesirable immigrants," Roosevelt proposed "a more rigid system of examination at our immigrant ports."

Although the new policy applied to all points of entry, of which there were more than three dozen, Ellis Island was the central concern. Because of its location in New York Harbor, it handled more arrivals than all the others combined. The numbers were staggering. A reporter described being overwhelmed by the presence of "nineteen hundred immigrants . . . in the buildings," only to be told by an immigration officer: "We sometimes have seven and eight thousand immigrants to handle at once and

The hospital was massive and modern—22 state-of-the-art buildings crammed onto two small islands, which were man-made from rock and dirt excavated during the building of the New York subway system. The first General Hospital building was Flemish-design brick with a limestone trim and large dormer windows. Construction began in 1900 and was completed a year later at a cost of about $33,000. Included in the medical complex was an autopsy amphitheater, a morgue, disinfecting areas, receiving and discharging rooms, and laundry facilities. Staff housing was provided on the second floor of the hospital.

then we have to work pretty hard. This year we expect a million immigrants."[10]

Recognizing that Ellis Island would need strong leadership if it was to institute a more thorough screening process, President Roosevelt turned to William Williams, a Wall Street lawyer who also happened to be a friend and a fellow veteran of the Spanish-American War. In some respects, Williams was an odd choice for Ellis Island commissioner. He was a millionaire whose roots traced to a signer of the Declaration of Independence, with little connection to the immigrants, who were new to America and most often dirt poor. When Edwin Moran died of tuberculosis soon after arriving at Ellis Island, his worldly possessions consisted of little more than a rosary and the $23.15 that were found in the pockets of his threadbare pants.[11] For his part, the bachelor Williams lived an opulent life at his suite in midtown Manhattan. As one newspaper wrote, Williams spent his daytime hours "over at Ellis Island, with all its squalor, its filth, its sorrow," but whiled away "his evenings in the luxury, the comfort, the elegance of the University Club."[12]

In his first directive as commissioner, Williams sought to curb the churlish reputation of Ellis Island's employees: "Immigrants shall be treated with kindness and civility by everyone at Ellis Island. Neither harsh language nor rough handling will be tolerated." Nevertheless, Williams had no particular affection for the new arrivals. True to his legal training and temperament, he was a stickler for rules. He insisted that immigration law be strictly applied: all able-bodied persons, and only the able-bodied, would be allowed entry. In response to a reporter's question as to whether "Italian organ grinders are of any practical, artistic or ethical value to the United States," Williams replied: "I don't see how they can be . . . and I would include peddlers with the organ grinders. Yet they come. We may know that they are to operate push carts and organs, but unless they are anarchists, convicted criminals, polygamists, idiots, epileptics, paupers, insane persons, are ill with some loathsome disease, or are likely to become charges upon the public, they must be admitted to the country."[13]

Soon after taking the commissioner's job, Williams saw that a more rigorous inspection process would require a state-of-the-art medical facility. "An enduring commonwealth," he said in a New

York City speech on the need for a new hospital, "must of necessity guard rigidly the health of its citizens and protect itself against undesirable additions from without."[14] Williams's goal seemed out of reach, however. Even if he could convince Congress to appropriate the money for a hospital, Ellis Island had no vacant land on which to build it.

Williams found his land in the tons of rocks that New York City was excavating as it built its subway system.

follows: "[W]ith an outside limit of 410 feet from the present island and with 200 feet of clear water space between the two islands, [the distance] would be amply sufficient to insure freedom from danger or contagion according to modern ideas of hospital construction."[16]

The first hospital in the Ellis Island complex—the General Hospital—opened on Island No. 2 in 1902. Connected to the main island by a 200-foot gangplank, it had 120 beds, making it larger than most city

{ "IMMIGRANTS SHALL BE TREATED WITH KINDNESS AND CIVILITY BY EVERYONE AT ELLIS ISLAND. NEITHER HARSH LANGUAGE NOR ROUGH HANDLING WILL BE TOLERATED." }

Secretary of Labor and Commerce V. H. Metcalf joined in: "We are about to build a hospital . . . but we must first build an island on which to place it."[15] There was, in fact, so much landfill available that *two* new islands were built next to the existing Ellis Island. Designated simply as Island No. 2 and Island No. 3, they were situated according to precise measurements. The Surgeon General of the United States defined the location of the island that would house the infectious disease hospital as

hospitals of the era. Even so, Commissioner Williams immediately complained to Washington officials that the new hospital's size was "utterly inadequate."[17] The General Hospital eventually would expand to 275 beds—more than three times the size of the typical city hospital. It included four operating rooms, a delivery room, and a morgue. Dr. Alfred C. Reed, a Public Health Service physician at the hospital, said of it: "A rare variety of diseases is seen. Patients literally from the farthest corners of the earth come together here. Rare tropical diseases, unusual internal disorders, strange skin lesions, as well as the more frequent cases of a busy general hospital present themselves here."[18]

After two mentally ill patients committed suicide in the general hospital, the Psychopathic Pavilion was built. It was charged with housing "idiots, imbeciles, feeble-minded persons, insane persons, and epileptics."[19] According to Thomas Salmon, an Ellis Island physician who helped design it, the Psychopathic Pavilion would make possible the "humane and efficient treatment to those immigrants who, during the voyage to America, become the victims of acute mental disorders."[20] Soon after it opened, however, the psychiatric hospital became a leading center of mental testing and, at the same time, an institution in which ideas about the mental inferiority of Italians, Slavs, and Jews flourished.

During William Williams's second term as commissioner, the third and

largest medical facility opened—the 450-bed Contagious Disease Hospital. Its construction was spurred by the previous commissioner, Robert Watchorn. Born of working-class parents in England, Watchorn was laboring in coal mines by the age of eleven. After reaching America as a young man, he worked his way up to become a labor organizer in Pennsylvania's coal fields before becoming an immigration official. Although Watchorn, like Williams, sought to restrict immigration to those fit for work, he never forgot his personal experience of being a newcomer. In a first encounter after his arrival, a Battery Park merchant shortchanged Watchorn and then had a beat cop drag him out of the store when Watchorn complained. Watchorn became Ellis Island commissioner after his exposé of New York's East Side sweatshops caught the attention of Washington, D.C., officials. The construction of an infectious disease hospital on Ellis Island reflected Watchorn's commitment to protecting arrivals from the sometimes callous indifference of their new countrymen.[21]

Located on Island No. 3, and more than 400 feet from the main island, the Contagious Disease Hospital, which opened in 1911, was the world's most advanced hospital of its kind. Boasting a mattress autoclave that could sterilize entire beds, it also had a refrigerator that held eight cadavers, an autopsy amphitheater that enabled visiting physicians and medical students to study the pathology of exotic diseases, and a sophisticated diagnostic laboratory staffed around the clock by a senior physician.[22]

The Contagious Disease Hospital had eighteen wards, each built to house patients with a particular disease. There were, for example, separate wards for whooping cough, measles, scarlet fever, favus, and diphtheria, and two wards each for trachoma and tuberculosis. Connected by a central corridor nearly two football fields in length, the wards had doors that were staggered to prevent air from one from easily entering another. The wards' size provided the exact cubic footage of air prescribed by the health guidelines of

Ellis Island was the first federal immigration station in the United States. In time, as many as sixty would line both coasts and the southern ports, but none would ever be as busy or as influential as Ellis Island. In 1892, the year it opened, Ellis Island received three out of every four immigrants seeking to enter the country.

Construction of the medical complex took nearly four years.
"The hospital building is of modern construction, on the block plan, of brick and stone construction, architecturally very handsome, and three stories and an attic in height, with a basement. The general plan of the building is a central portion for executive and administrative purposes, with wings containing large and small wards." REPORT BY ASSISTANT SURGEON GENERAL H. D. GEDDINGS, 1906

the time, and each was ventilated by banks of windows, maximizing airflow between the interior and exterior, while minimizing the flow between wards. The Contagious Disease Hospital had its own laundry—upward of 3,000 sheets and towels were washed and dried there each day.[23]

When fully completed, the hospital complex also included 19 other buildings. Heat, light, and power for the hospital were furnished by the power plant on the first island. Sewage flowed, by force of gravity,

into New York Harbor. The kitchen alone was a large enterprise—2,000 meals a day were prepared by its cooking staff. All told, 300 people worked in the Ellis Island hospital complex, about a third of them medical doctors, nurses, and orderlies, many of whom lived in staff housing on the island.[24]

Few hospitals in America were as imposing as the one on Ellis Island. New York's Bellevue Hospital, which had started as a public almshouse, began an expansion

Steamship companies had exterminators on board the ships to help control the rats, a common carrier of disease.
  "*Certain diseases are found so frequently among immigrants, and others are so inherently dangerous, as to merit special mention because of their important relation to public health. . . . There is a constant stream of fresh infection pouring in.*"
DR. ALFRED C. REED, U.S. PUBLIC HEALTH SERVICE, 1912

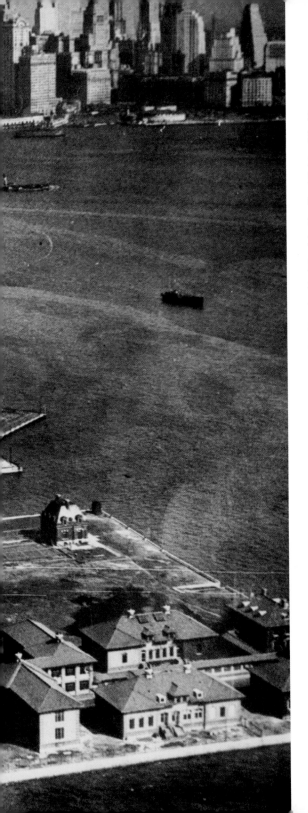

in the same decade as the Ellis Island hospital was built and eventually grew to 3,000 beds, making it the country's largest. Its private rival, the New York Hospital, also underwent a massive expansion during this period.[25] But no hospital could match Ellis Island's in the array of diseases and patients it handled. Milton Foster, one of its physicians, noted: "It is by no means unusual to receive one hundred cases or more at the hospital in one day. The task of admitting, examining, treating, and housing this number of new patients in five or six hours, would tax the capacity of the largest hospitals in the country. Here the problem is also complicated by the fact that practically none of the patients speak English."[26] Upon visiting the hospital in 1922, Sir Auckland Geddes, the British ambassador to the United States, saw fit to remark: "The hospital . . . has to deal with every sort of disorder, ranging from slight injury to obscure tropical disease. It is at once a maternity home and an insane asylum."[27]

"Ellis Island is a good sized city. Some days there are as many as 10,000 people temporarily or permanently upon the island." FREDERIC C. HOWE, COMMISSIONER OF IMMIGRATION, 1916

Women and children use the sinks at Ellis Island to wash up. Many immigrant families spent several days on the island waiting for their medical and legal inspections to be completed before they could enter the mainland.

"They got off the boat and then they walked in, in a parade, up those stairs into the building. . . . Many of them came through with all of their bedding and belongings . . . their last possessions, you know, that they owned. And they looked pretty bad."

SALLY LOTH, HEBREW IMMIGRANT AID SOCIETY, 1914–1918

17

"The nurses, the ladies in white, we used to call them. They were very nice. They talked to the children. They stroked their hair, and they touched their cheeks and held our hands."

ELIZABETH MARTIN, IMMIGRANT FROM HUNGARY, 1920

A young patient sits on the steps of the Ellis Island Hospital with Public Health Service nurse Jennie Colligan, who went by the nickname "Mother."

Greeting the immigrants, once they'd passed through the quarantine station, were doctors from the United States Marine Hospital Service. Created in 1798 to care for merchant seamen abroad, the Marine Hospital Service had evolved, by the 1890s, into a small and highly disciplined corps of medical elite that would soon be known by its modern name, the U.S. Public Health Service.

"I never heard any of the medical officers discuss immigration laws. That was something that was not in our line and there was no indication of the need of discussing these laws. We did what we thought was right to the best of our ability."

DR. GROVER KEMPF,
U.S. PUBLIC HEALTH SERVICE, 1912

Ellis Island Hospital laboratory. When it came to infectious diseases such as tuberculosis, Commissioner Williams depended on the hospital's state-of-the-art laboratory to determine whether an immigrant would be deported or not. "No case of pulmonary tuberculosis will be certified as 'dangerous contagious,' unless the clinical symptoms are well marked and the tubercle bacillus has been found in the sputum." WILLIAM WILLIAMS, REPORT TO THE SURGEON GENERAL

Before the Contagious Disease Hospital opened on Ellis Island in 1911, immigrants, including many children, who were exposed to or suffering from virulent diseases were separated from their families and quarantined on neighboring harbor islands. Ernst Lederle, then New York City health commissioner, explained: "The patients from Ellis Island should not be brought into the city limits at all. They are a source of infection from the time they leave the island until they reach the foot of East Sixteenth Street."

"No law has been enacted to prevent the strong, the willing, the honest, the moral, or the healthy from landing, only certain classes are denied the right to come among us and take residence here. The proscription of these classes is intended to sift, rather than to restrict, immigration."

TERRENCE POWDERLY, COMMISSIONER GENERAL OF IMMIGRATION, 1902

esident Roosevelt visits Ellis Island, Sept. 16, 1903

Editorial cartoons filled the pages of local and national newspapers during the great wave of immigration. Many called for further restrictions on immigrants, as Italians and Jews replaced the inflow of immigrants from northern Europe. "A strict execution of our present laws makes it possible to keep out what may be termed the worst riff-raff of Europe," proclaimed William Williams, Ellis Island commissioner of immigration.

25

And Still They Come.

By J. Campbell Cory.

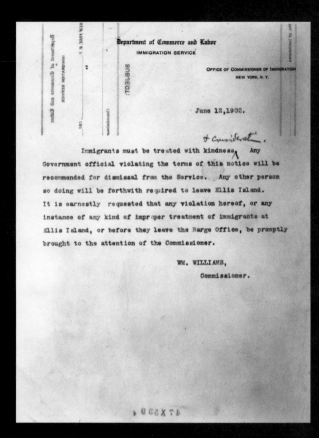

June 12,1902.

Immigrants must be treated with kindness. Any Government official violating the terms of this notice will be recommended for dismissal from the Service. Any other person so doing will be forthwith required to leave Ellis Island. It is earnestly requested that any violation hereof, or any instance of any kind of improper treatment of immigrants at Ellis Island, or before they leave the Barge Office, be promptly brought to the attention of the Commissioner.

WM. WILLIAMS,
Commissioner.

In his first memo as commissioner of immigration, William Williams set a tone of civility, writing, "Immigrants shall be treated with kindness and consideration by everyone at Ellis Island. Neither harsh language nor rough handling will be tolerated. The Commissioner desires that any instance of disobedience of this order be brought immediately to his attention."

Editorial cartoon spoofing the increasing numbers of immigrants arriving daily at Ellis Island, 1908. "The immigrant per se has no moral or social right to enter this country against the will of its citizens. An enduring commonwealth must of necessity guard rigidly the health of its citizens and protect itself against undesirable additions from without."

DR. ALFRED C. REED, U.S. PUBLIC HEALTH SERVICE, 1912

Frederick Rothe, along with his son Frederick and wife Theresa. Frederick Rothe was an interpreter at Ellis Island until his death from tuberculosis in 1915. He was the only employee known to become infected with a contagious disease while working with the immigrants. It took his wife ten years to collect her husband's death benefits from the federal government.

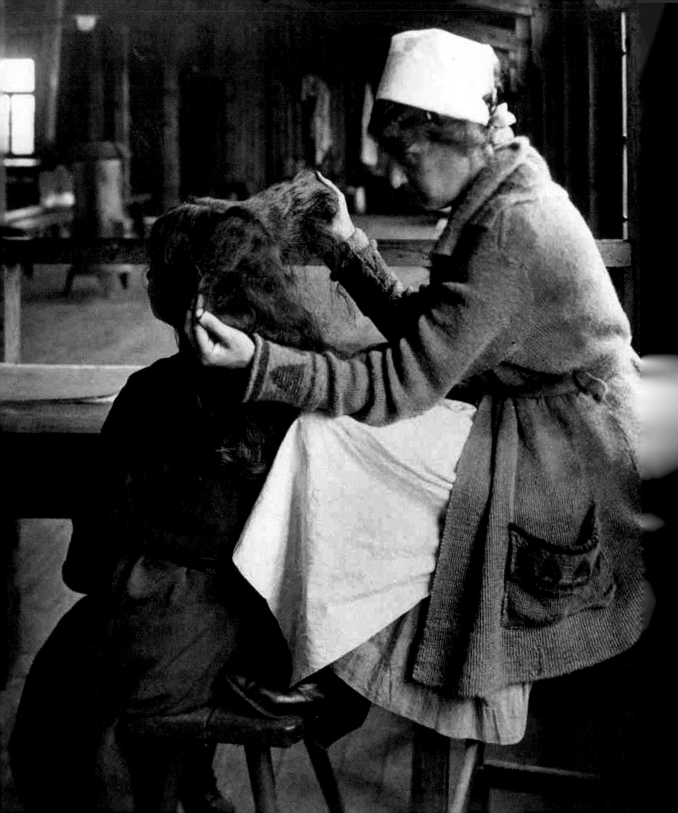

CHAPTER 2

WALKING THE LINE

"THERE'S A CONSTANT STREAM OF FRESH INFECTION POURING IN."[1]

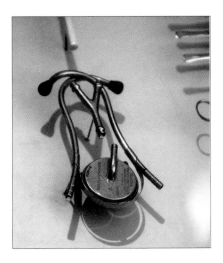

"The doctors examine each immigrant for one of 17 diseases that have to be watched against, such as favus, which attacks the head and finger-nails. When the doctor finds disease, he chalk-marks the case . . . and, if there was no disease, let the man or woman pass to the next pen."

THE SPECTATOR (ANONYMOUS),
Outlook Magazine, March 1905

inspection line, a medical officer examined his eyes and wrote "Ct" in chalk on his shirt, directing him to step to the side. Theodore Kelsch had trachoma, a contagious eye disease that causes blindness and was grounds for deportation.[2]

Each day at Ellis Island, nearly 2,000 new arrivals climbed the most fateful staircase of their lives. A uniformed officer of the Public Health Service (PHS) stood at the top landing, watching intently. As the passengers scaled the steps, lugging their suitcases, the officer looked for the slightest indication of poor health. Upon reaching the top, the passengers were handed a medical card and directed to the left or right, depending on whether they were being processed in the registry's south or north hall. Once there, they stood in line until it was their turn to come forward, each step studied by a uniformed doctor who then examined the scalp, hands, eyes, and throat.[3]

The inspection process was like an assembly line.[4] Every ten seconds or so, another passenger was instructed to step forward. A chalk mark was swiped across the clothing of anyone suspected of carrying a disease. One physician called it "a haphazard method of examination but . . . the only way that it could be done, as we were running about 2,500 immigrants a day."[5] Even the turns in the inspection line had a purpose. Said Dr. Victor Safford: "We used to like to have passengers while under inspection make two right angle turns, the scheme served to bring the light on both sides of a passenger's face. The turns also helped bring out imperfections in muscular coordination."[6]

As a result of inspecting hundreds of immigrants a day, Ellis Island's physicians developed a keen diagnostic ability. Frederick Haskin, a journalist who spent days observing the medical inspections, wrote: "While the immigrant has been walking the twenty feet, the doctors have asked and answered in their own mind several hundred questions. If the immigrant reveals any intimation of disease, if he has a deformity, even down to a crooked finger, the fact is noticed. If he is also so evidently a healthy person that their examination reveals no reason why he should be held, he is passed on. But if there is the least suspicion in the minds of the doctors that there is anything wrong with him, a chalk mark is placed upon the lapel of his coat."[7]

Haskin's observations accorded with those of Broughton Brandenburg, a journalist who posed as an immigrant in order to walk through the inspection line. "An old man who limped in front of me," wrote Brandenburg, "was marked with a bit of chalk on the coat lapel."[8]

Word of the strict medical inspection had reached Europe, and arrivals did their best to hide afflictions. Writing in *Popular Science Monthly* in 1905, Dr. Allan McLaughlin noted: "The medical examiners must ever be on the alert for deception. The nonchalant individual with an overcoat on his arm is probably concealing an artificial arm; the child strapped to its mother's back, and who appears old enough to walk alone, may be unable to walk because of infantile paralysis; a case of favus may be so skillfully prepared for inspection that close scrutiny is required to detect the evidences of recent cleansing. . . ."

Immigrants who could afford first- or second-class passage and were therefore

A Public Health Service nurse examines an immigrant for hair lice. This examination was preceded by a shower, spraying with delousing powder, and clothes being washed and sterilized.

"I remember crying. My mother had to push me to go there with this nurse and they sprayed us or whatever. All our clothes were off and the clothes were steamed . . . and then they would shake them . . . and we'd put them on." ELIZABETH MARTIN, IMMIGRANT FROM HUNGARY, 1920

presumed fit to become Americans went through a speedy inspection line that included a cursory medical exam. Close scrutiny was reserved for the poor passengers who traveled in steerage and were expected to take factory jobs.[9] Roughly one in five of these arrivals was pulled out of the line for a fuller medical examination. Seventeen conditions, ranging from problems of the eyes to weaknesses of physique, could result in detention.

Immigrants with infectious diseases such as measles, mumps, diphtheria, and whooping cough were sent to the Ellis Island Hospital for what was usually a short stay. When five-year-old John Gaquer arrived from France, his throat was inflamed from a tonsil operation earlier that year. Unwilling to accept that explanation, however, the PHS doctors sent him to the hospital. "They thought I had diphtheria or the beginnings of diphtheria, which was at

> { "THEY CANNOT UNDERSTAND BY WHAT STROKE OF SCURVY FORTUNE THEY HAVE BEEN SELECTED FROM AMONG ALL THE OTHERS AND FORBIDDEN TO ENTER THE PROMISED LAND." }

"Class A" conditions, which included trachoma, were cause for deportation. The process could be unnerving. "They cannot understand by what stroke of scurvy fortune they have been selected from among all the others and forbidden to enter the Promised Land," said PHS physician Milton Foster. "The more excitable burst into tears, wring their hands, and protest loudly against this great and unexpected injustice. It is useless to try to calm or reassure them."[10]

epidemic stage at that time in New York. And I guess to play it safe, they sent me to the hospital in isolation."[11]

Other arrivals went to the hospital without much hope of a cure. When 22-year-old Pearl Yablonski went through the line, her dull expression caught the attention of the examining physician, who asked: "How many feet does a horse have?" Pearl's family would later claim that she did not answer because she thought the question was stupid. But after psychiatric testing at the hospital, she was diagnosed as feebleminded and shipped back to Romania.[12]

The medical inspection at Ellis Island was conducted by order of Congress. Diseases that scarcely get passing notice today were life-threatening in 1900. Measles was easily spread and could be fatal. Life expectancy in America was only 48 years of age for whites and a mere 33 years for blacks. The PHS physicians at Ellis Island were "guardians of the gate"— the nation's first line of defense against immigrant-borne illness. As Ellis Island commissioner William Williams noted at a conference in New York: "The importance of the medical side [cannot be overstated]. . . . Medical officers of the U.S. Public Health Service . . . are expected to detect and report to the immigration authorities all disease, physical and mental, that immigrants may bring."[13] Even so, disease slipped through. When polio broke out in the Italian section of Brooklyn in 1916, frightened residents blamed it on a recent immigrant. Dr. Charles Lavinder acknowledged the possibility: "Cases might develop on board during the voyage and contacts, incubating the disease, might

"Specially examined and passed." When stamped on an inspection card, this meant the immigrant was close to departing Ellis Island as a new citizen.

easily pass inspection at Ellis Island, to develop the infection later at their point of destination."[14]

Fifteen years after Ellis Island opened, growing opposition to immigration led Congress to expand the authority of the Public Health Service, requiring it to weed out the weak and the unemployable as well as the sick. The new list of conditions marking one for exclusion included "likely to become a public charge"—meaning someone who had little hope of finding a job. This was a Class A condition—cause for deportation. The head of the Bureau of Immigration, Terrence Powderly, was among those calling for stricter standards. "There exists no reason," Powderly claimed, "why the United States should become the hospital of the nations of the earth."[15]

Public health was not the only thing on Commissioner Powderly's mind. In the 1890s, as head of the powerful Knights of Labor, he had railed against the large numbers of immigrants coming into the country, telling a congressional committee that they "lived like beasts" and were taking jobs that belonged to Americans.[16] Ellis Island's physicians accepted their legal obligation to weed out the medically unfit. Said Dr. Milton Foster of the Public Health Service: "The medical inspection of arriving immigrants is made chiefly for two purposes: first, to see that they are strong, well, and bright enough to be able to earn a living and get along in this country; and second, to ascertain that they did not have certain diseases that they might transmit to their new neighbors in America."[17]

Immigrants could be excluded for political, moral, or economic reasons as well. Suspected criminals, anarchists, military deserters, prostitutes, and polygamists were among those barred from entry, as were paupers whom a foreign government had given a steamship ticket in order to get rid of them. But poor health was the most common basis for deportation.[18] Any immigrant certified as unhealthy was at risk, though some PHS physicians preferred to downplay the role of their diagnoses. "It is not within the province of the medical officers to pass judgment on the eligibility of the immigrant for admission," wrote Dr. Alfred C. Reed. "The medical certificate merely states the diagnosis, leaving to the immigration inspector in the registry division the duty of deciding the question of admission."[19]

As medical doctors, the PHS physicians followed an oath to heal all patients. As

With an "X" chalk-marked on their jacket or dress, nine out of 100 immigrants at Ellis Island were separated for further mental testing.

"Justice to the immigrant requires a carefully considered diagnosis; while on the other hand, the interests of this country demand an unremitting search for the insane persons among the hundreds of thousands of immigrants who present themselves annually at our ports of entry." DR. THOMAS SALMON, U.S. PUBLIC HEALTH SERVICE, 1905

uniformed officers of the Public Health Service, they were obliged to identify the medically unfit.[20] Which imperative should govern? The available evidence, though largely anecdotal, suggests that most PHS doctors adhered to the strictures of the law while showing leniency when possible. Dr. Alfred C. Reed claimed: "Seldom, indeed, does the alien suffer from too harsh a medical judgment."[21] An exemplary case was that of 13-year-old Dante Pavoggi, who was diagnosed in 1911 with "chronic inflammation of glands of the neck" that could inhibit his "ability to earn a living." Instead of being deported, Dante was allowed to join his uncle in rural Illinois: "The fact that this boy is destined to a farm, rather than a congested city, is very much

in his favor. With good air, the suitable environments, he will very likely recover."[22]

Although a chalk mark could signal the start of the deportation process, it ordinarily led to a less severe outcome. A limp or hacking cough by itself was not a barrier to entry. But some exclusionary conditions like "poor physique" were imprecise, allowing for liberal interpretation by inspectors. What were the symptoms of "poor physique" that foretold an immigrant's inability to hold a job? According to immigration records, Izie Friegel, a 24-year-old Russian Jew, had sufficiently serious symptoms. In 1910, when Friegel left his wife, child, and a job as a tailor in Russia, he had just 22 dollars in his pocket and the promise from a nephew to meet him in New York City. During his medical inspection, though, Friegel was diagnosed as having a "flat chest and malnutrition," and was deported as someone "likely to become a public charge."

Nowhere was the law more convoluted than when it came to employment. Immigrants who arrived with the firm promise of a job other than in a family business could be denied entry on those grounds alone. By law, immigrants had to compete for work with those already here. Yet immigrants also could be denied entry if for health reasons their chance of finding employment was slim. As a result, the fate of an immigrant could rest with the medical diagnosis. If an immigrant was certified as physically able to work, the odds of admission were high. The case of Izie Friegel notwithstanding, PHS physicians usually sided with the immigrant, despite periodic complaints from immigration officials that their judgments were too lenient. Gertrude Slaughter, one of the first woman physicians to serve at Ellis Island, observed: "I approached my task with considerable misgiving, feeling that I had become part of the crushing mechanism. I soon learned, however, that although I was one of the watchdogs at the gate, I was expected to show as much kindness and consideration as possible."[23]

Some diseases, however, were too threatening to the public health to be overlooked. Trachoma was among them. One of the oldest diseases in recorded history, trachoma is spread by human contact, and its initial symptoms are reddening of the eye and bumps on the interior of the eyelid. As the disease advances, the eyelid scars, causing the upper lid to turn inward, leading the eyelashes to brush against the cornea, gradually scarring it and leading to blindness.

According to oral histories obtained from Ellis Island immigrants, no aspect of the medical inspection was more unpleasant than the trachoma exam. "Button shoes were common in those days, and there was

on President Theodore Roosevelt during his tour of Ellis Island. Upon returning to the White House, he sent an urgent letter to the Public Health Service: "I was struck by the way in which the doctors made the examinations with dirty hands and with no pretense to clean their instruments, so that it would seem to me that these examinations so conducted would themselves be a fruitful source of

{ "I SOON LEARNED . . . THAT ALTHOUGH I WAS ONE OF THE WATCHDOGS AT THE GATE, I WAS EXPECTED TO SHOW AS MUCH KINDNESS AND CONSIDERATION AS POSSIBLE." }

a little loop to button shoes that was used to turn the eyelid—it was the most efficient way of turning the eyes ever devised," said Dr. Grover Kempf, who used the technique as did many of his colleagues.[24] Kempf noted that other physicians simply grabbed the eyelid, turning it inside out with their fingers: "The method used was to have a towel soaked in Lysol solution over your shoulder, and each time you examined the patient you wiped your fingers and hands with the solution."[25]

The eye exam made a strong impression

carrying infection from diseased to healthy persons."[26]

Fiorello La Guardia, who worked as an interpreter on Ellis Island and later became New York City's mayor, saw the trachoma exam differently. "Several hundred immigrants daily were found to be suffering from trachoma, and their exclusion was mandatory," wrote La Guardia. "It was harrowing to see families separated because the precaution had not been taken of [examining them in their home country]. Sometimes, if it was

INSPECTION OF SUSPECTS FOR SKIN DISEASES, ETC.—ALL EMIGRANTS ARE
INATED BEFORE THEY LEAVE THEIR NATIVE LAND, AND ARE EXAMINED EACH
DAY BY THE DOCTOR ON BOARD THE SHIP AS THEIR CARDS SHOW.

"I think frankly the worst memory I have of Ellis Island was the physical because the doctors were seated at a long table with a basin full of potassium chloride and you had to stand in front of them. . . . And you had to reveal yourself. . . . Right there in front of everyone, I mean, it wasn't private! It's a very unpleasant memory." MANNY STEEN, IMMIGRANT FROM IRELAND, 1925

a young child who suffered from trachoma, one of the parents had to return to the native country with the rejected member of the family. When they learned their fate, they were stunned. They had never felt ill. They had never heard the word trachoma. They could see all right, and they had no homes to return to. I suffered because I was so powerless to help these poor people."[27]

Although debilitating diseases like trachoma prompted numerous deportations, most immigrants with Class A conditions were healed at patient expense at the Ellis Island Hospital.[28] In some cases, a hospital stay was made possible through the intervention of immigrant aid groups. Sally Loth, a case worker with the Hebrew Immigrant Aid Society, recalled the many petitions that her group filed on behalf of diseased immigrants. "We were making briefs out all the time," said Loth. "I was typing and typing to make these briefs out, and they were on long legal paper, giving the government reasons why this family should stay and why that little boy should be allowed to be treated at Ellis Island."[29]

Thousands of patients had their treatment paid for in whole or part by aid groups and, in some cases, by government itself. One such patient was the 15-year-old German boy Theodore Kelsch, described at the start of this chapter as having a "Ct" marked on his clothing in chalk as he passed through the inspection line. After his father agreed to pay the costs, Theodore was admitted to the Ellis Island Hospital

for treatment of his trachoma. However, his father ran out of money eight weeks later, leading him to file this plea with the Board of Special Inquiry:

Please help a German-American out of an embarrassing situation. . . . I am not in a position to pay for all of this, having paid his fare as a cabin passenger and his board in Germany. I earn $18 a week, and had saved $300 but now all my money is gone and I have to look out also for my family here. I am willing to pay something, but can not possibly raise so much. It would beggar me. I have always been a good citizen, have never been arrested, and have been a foreman ever since I am in this country. I think my son belongs to us, and he will make a good citizen.

The Board granted the father's request, and Theodore's care was paid for through a general fund supported by a head tax on immigrants. Three months after he was hospitalized, Theodore Kelsch was pronounced cured and reunited with his father.[30]

In 1907, an anonymous journalist who went by the name The Spectator described a visit to Ellis Island: "Thirteen ships had come in that day, and nineteen hundred immigrants were in the buildings; but this, the official informed The Spectator as he conducted him up to the visitors' gallery, was not a particularly busy day. 'We sometimes have seven and eight thousand immigrants to handle at once,' he said, 'and then we have to work pretty hard. This year we expect a million immigrants.'"

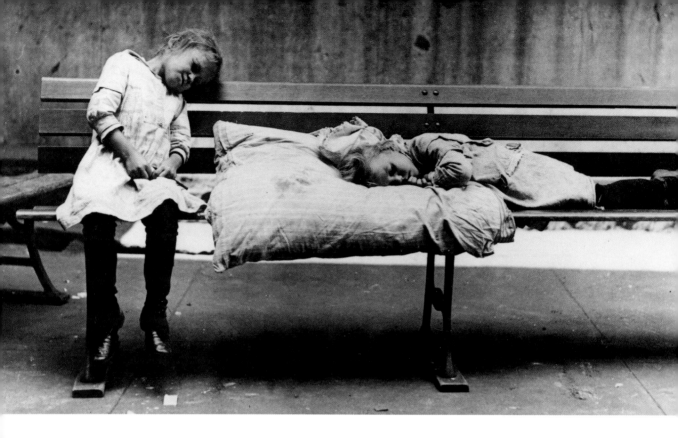

"Half-way up the stairs an interpreter stood telling the immigrants to get their health tickets ready. . . . The majority of the people, having their hands full of bags, boxes, bundles, and children, carried their tickets in their teeth, and just at the head of the stairs stood a young doctor in the Marine Hospital Service uniform who took them, looked at them, and stamped them with the Ellis Island stamp. . . ." JOURNALIST BROUGHTON BRANDENBURG, 1904

"In the middle, facing the gallery, was a stairway, coming up from below somewhere, and up this gangway poured an unceasing stream of immigrants, two or three abreast. Most of the men had small trunks on their heads or shoulders; the women wore shawls or handkerchiefs on their heads, and led or carried small children. They came up, stolidly, steadily, submissively, like so many cattle. . . ."

THE SPECTATOR, 1907

Childhood diseases like mumps, chicken pox, and measles were common among the immigrant children at Ellis Island. In an era before antibiotics, these diseases could be fatal. After being diagnosed, children were separated from their parents and sent to the hospital for care.

"I was put in a little wagon, like a handcart, and pushed across a sort of bridge, a narrow bridge with windows on each side, and taken to the hospital there and plunked down on the bed. . . ." FLORA GREENWALD, IMMIGRANT FROM POLAND, 1922

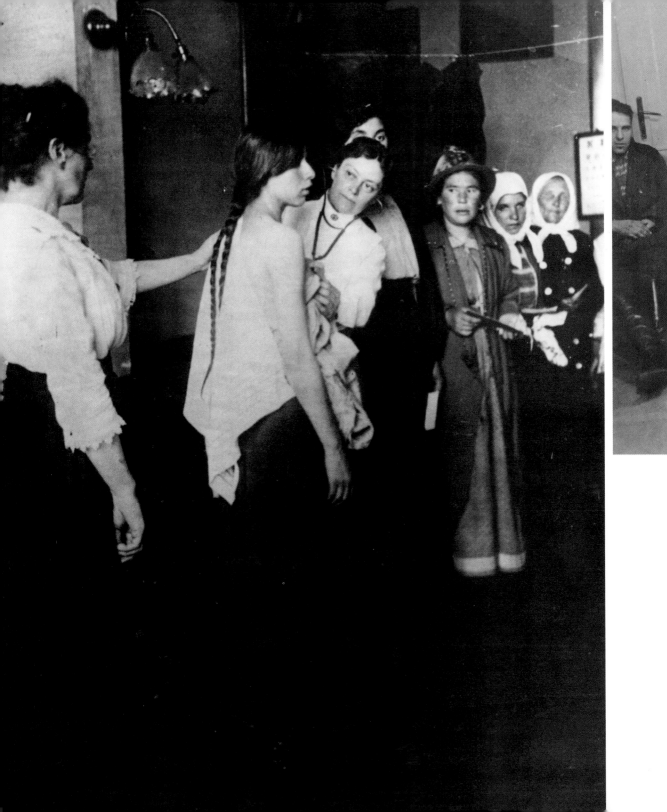

Immigrants awaiting inspection.

"We should unquestionably be more particular than we are as to whom we receive and strive for quality rather than quantity. We require only immigrants of the right sort, those who are physically strong and who possess such moral and other qualities as will help build up the race and the nation." WILLIAM WILLIAMS, COMMISSIONER OF IMMIGRATION, 1910

"We went to this big, open room, and there were a couple of doctors there, and they tell you, 'Strip.' And my mother had never, ever undressed in front of us. In those days nobody would. She was so embarrassed. . . ."

ENID GRIFFITHS JONES, IMMIGRANT FROM WALES, 1923

47

Immigrants faced legal and social questions during the inspection process.

"The questions were, 'Did you get married just to come to the United States?' Then, 'How long are you married? Have you any children? How old are the children? Have you had any differences with your wife? Do you get along all right? . . .'"   DR. ROBERT LESLIE, U.S. PUBLIC HEALTH SERVICE, 1912

Mothers traveling alone with their children were not released from Ellis Island until a husband or relative came to meet them. Immigration authorities required that legal documents be signed by these individuals guaranteeing financial support of the family to prevent them from becoming future "public charges."

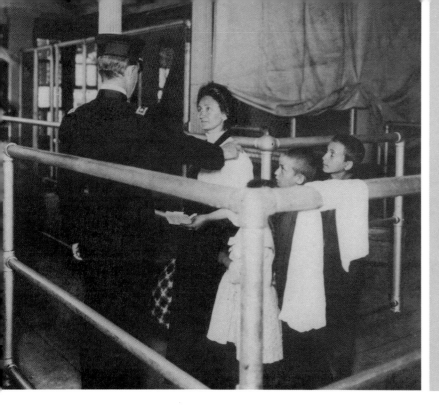

A mother and her children await
an eye examination. Doctors were
checking for trachoma, a contagious
disease that can lead to blindness.
Many immigrants were unaware that
they had this incurable eye condition.
In his memoir about working on Ellis
Island, Dr. Victor Heiser wrote, "Ours
would be the painful duty of singling
out one of the children, and of saying,
'She has trachoma. She cannot enter.'
The mother and the rest of the children
would have to return to Europe
with the diseased one, and until the
boat sailed, the father, wretched and
unhappy, would haunt the detention
quarters, while his family kept up a
constant wailing and crying."

"The medical inspection of arriving immigrants is made chiefly for two
purposes; first, to see that they are strong, well, and bright enough to be able
to earn a living and get along in this country; and second, to ascertain that
they do not have certain diseases which they might transmit to their new
neighbors in America."

A GENERAL HOSPITAL FOR ALL NATIONS,
DR. MILTON FOSTER, U.S. PUBLIC HEALTH SERVICE, 1915

Physicians from the U.S. Public Health Service. A rotation through Ellis Island was mandatory for all PHS doctors given the experience it offered. Most preferred to work in the hospital instead of conducting medical inspections.

"The line work was considered a hardship by the older doctors."

DR. GROVER KEMPF, 1912

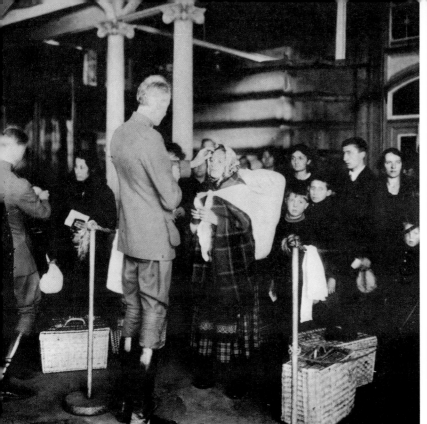

"Close by the door stood a physician who pounced upon the heads of the passing immigrants and pulled them toward him, rumpled their hair, and peered closely at the scalp for favus. . . . The next inspector has acquired an amazing speed and accuracy. He stands directly in the path of the approaching immigrant, holding a little stick in his hand. By a quick movement and the force of his own compelling gaze, he catches the eyes of his subject and holds them. You will see the immigrant stop short, lift his head with a quick jerk, and open his eyes very wide. The inspector reaches with a swift movement, catches the eyelash with his thumb and finger, turns it back, and peers under it."

THE SPECTATOR, 1908

"Not realizing that they are sick, they cannot understand by what stroke of scurvy fortune they have been selected from among all the others and forbidden to enter the Promised Land. The more excitable burst into tears, wring their hands, and protest loudly against this great and unexpected injustice. It is useless to try to calm or reassure them."

A GENERAL HOSPITAL FOR ALL NATIONS,

DR. MILTON FOSTER, U.S. PUBLIC HEALTH SERVICE, 1915

"I remember coming into a long, dark room with very long tables of bare wood. It had wooden benches not chairs. We heard lots of languages from all kinds of family groups. You had to share these tables—there weren't enough tables so people could be private. . . . But it really didn't matter because we were all in the same boat—everybody was miserable."

LEAH SHAIN, NIECE OF PEARL
YABLONSKI, AN IMMIGRANT
FROM ROMANIA, 1921

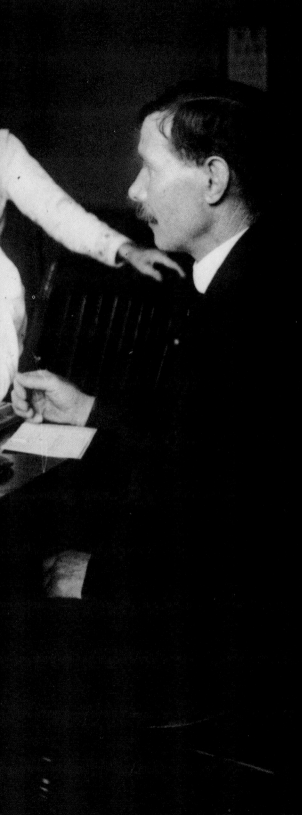

"*Each immigrant should be given one or two performance tests. There are a number of these tests, some of them very simple and others more difficult. The number in which the subject attempts to solve them throws considerable light on his general intelligence.*" DR. EUGENE H. MULLAN, U.S. PUBLIC HEALTH SERVICE, 1917

 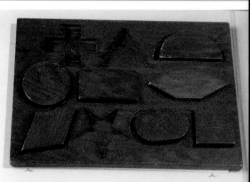

Seguin formboard.
The improvement time was the most important factor in this test.
Completion time for a 9-year-old: 20 seconds.

"The mental examination of immigrants was always haphazard. It couldn't be any other way because of the time given to pass the immigrants along the line."

DR. GROVER KEMPF, U.S. PUBLIC

HEALTH SERVICE, 1912

63

Ellis Island Immigration Service interpreters (Fiorello La Guardia can be seen in the upper left corner).
   "It is often asked if the hospital has a large corps of interpreters, and if not, how it is possible to properly diagnose and treat the ailments of those with whom the physicians cannot talk. As a matter of fact, there are no interpreters employed especially for the hospital. Some of the physicians and employees can speak one or more foreign languages, and all of the staff have picked up a few useful words in several tongues. When it becomes absolutely necessary, an interpreter is borrowed from the regular corps employed by the immigration service." A GENERAL HOSPITAL FOR ALL NATIONS, DR. MILTON FOSTER, U.S. PUBLIC HEALTH SERVICE, 1915

Fiorello La Guardia, law school graduation photo. The future mayor of New York City worked as an interpreter at Ellis Island from 1907 to 1910 while attending law school at night. Patients in the hospital remember his visits.

"*I caught the disease trachoma. I failed my examination. My mother and sister were allowed to disembark, and I was sent to the Ellis Island Hospital for further treatment, which stretched to 17 months. . . . I received a periodic visit from a short, round-face man, who always brought me a bar of Runkels chocolate. He was the island's interpreter in Yiddish, Italian, and Spanish. I believe he was La Guardia.*" EXCERPT FROM A LETTER WRITTEN BY LOUIS K. PITMAN, MD, AN IMMIGRANT FROM JERUSALEM, 1907

The Red Cross and other immigrant aid societies were eager to help the immigrants look more "American" before they left Ellis Island. With clothes donated by wealthy New Yorkers, many women received a new outfit and a "dash of powder," or makeup, before being met by their husbands.

"All races and conditions of men come together here and adjust themselves more or less amicably to each other. Children with no common bond of race, language, or religion play together perhaps more happily for that very reason. Some have been here for months." THE SPECTATOR, 1907

A brother and sister are cleared to leave Ellis Island. The tags pinned to their chests indicate their destination.

For many
immigrants,
the medical
and mental
inspection
made the
experience of
Ellis Island a
harrowing one.

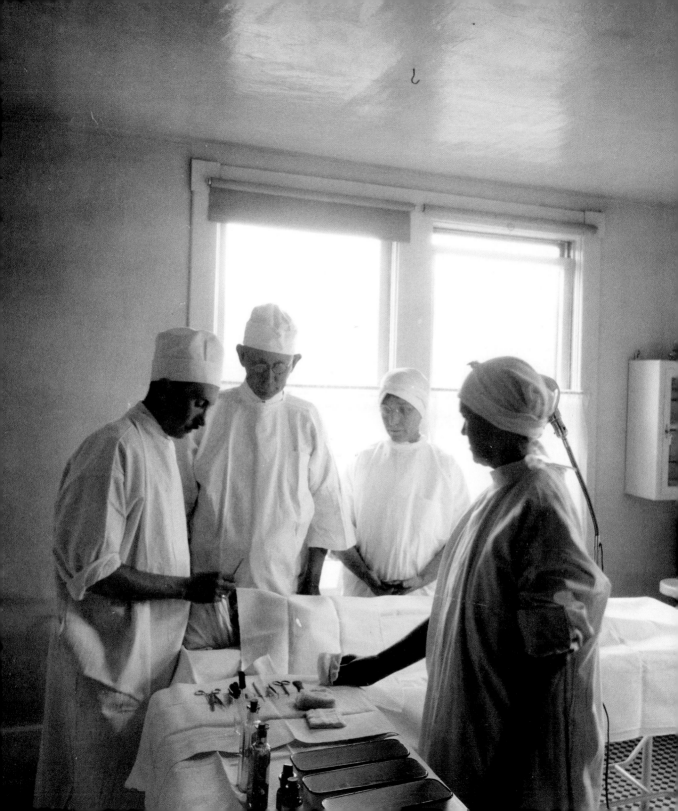

CHAPTER 3

TREATING PATIENTS BY THE THOUSANDS

"ADMIT, NOT REJECT."[1]

"In the hospital . . . we were actually doing work that we were supposed to do by our training—that is, treat sick people."

DR. GROVER KEMPF,
Ellis Island physician

S THEY WERE REMOVED FROM THE INSPECTION LINE FOR
FAILURE TO PASS THE MEDICAL EXAM, IMMIGRANTS WERE WALKED
OR WHEELED TO THE HOSPITAL. FEAR WAS A COMMON REACTION,

particularly among children. "I was five years and five months old," recalled John Gaquer, a French immigrant introduced in chapter 2. "I didn't know what was happening to me. They took me away from my mother . . . and here I was in this place not knowing if I was going to see her again."[2] Ten-year-old Josephine Messina Cirella, who spent 23 days at the hospital without seeing her parents, worried they had "forgot me" and thought authorities were planning to send her back to Sicily.[3]

Ellis Island physicians also had cause for worry. They were vaccinated against smallpox and typhus fever, but these were only two of the life-threatening diseases they faced. Other diseases, though less serious, were unnerving. Barber's Itch—or folliculitis—is a form of ringworm that causes blistering, crusting, and oozing in the lower facial region. Easily spread by touch, its victims have a maddening urge to scratch the infected area. Bruce Anderson, a staff physician at Ellis Island, remarked: "Barber's Itch impressed me so much I have never been able to allow anyone fooling around my face."[4]

Few hospitals had as large a patient load as the one on Ellis Island. In a 1915 article, staff physician Dr. Milton Foster compared the hospital's workload to that of all hospitals in Boston and Washington, D.C. "Take any week in the year and imagine that, during this week, all the people who were sick and needed treatment in [the two cities] were to be sent to one hospital," wrote Dr. Foster. "Assume, also, that this hospital was a real general hospital, in the fullest sense of the word, and that it accepted not only ordinary patients but also the insane and those suffering from contagious diseases. Let us also further suppose that all the [residents of the two cities] were inspected and that all those who were suspected of having latent disorders, like tuberculosis or syphilis, were also sent to this hospital for examination and treatment. Grant all of these conditions and you will have a pretty fair idea of the total amount of work performed by the hospital at Ellis Island last year."[5]

Upon admission to the hospital, patients were forced to bathe, having just spent three weeks in a crowded steerage compartment. Some patients loathed bathing or had hidden reasons for resisting. As Josephine Lutomski, a ward matron, explained: "Some of the patients would get very nasty if you tried to take their clothes from them. They thought you were stealing their clothes. And then we found out why. Some of them had money sewed in their hems, the bills, and even in the seams they had the money rolled up in the seams of their clothes. One person wouldn't take her hat off. She wore it like this bed cap . . . her bills [were] sewed in there."[6]

Stubbornness or ignorance could delay an immigrant's release from the hospital. A 1920 Red Cross report told of a Polish peasant woman named Basha who refused to undress for an X-ray to determine whether her persistent cough was caused by tuberculosis. "She was very angry at being detained and was depressed and sulky. . . . For days the doctor had been trying to have an X-ray taken of her lungs but she not only refused but behaved so strangely that he was seriously considering certifying her insane." Basha would not speak or listen to anyone, even the interpreter. When she finally spoke, her thinking revealed itself. She was convinced that the X-ray machine was a camera that police were using to obtain a nude photograph. "I am not a bad woman," she said. "And I won't have any photograph taken with no clothes on." After the purpose of the X-ray was explained, she agreed to it, insisting that the ward matron remain with her during the procedure. The X-ray results were negative, and she was released.[7]

Privacy was in short supply at the hospital. Patients were housed in open

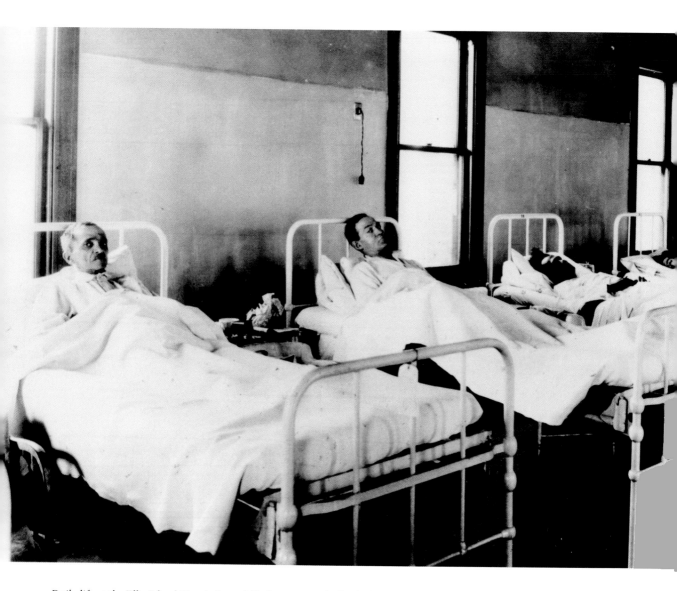

Daily life at the Ellis Island Hospital was full of surprises—for both the patient and the medical staff. Dr. Victor Safford recalled a time when a Bulgarian patient flew into a rage after the attendant brought him a bathrobe: "The attendant thought that the man had gone insane. A patient a few beds away who understood the Bulgarian . . . laughingly explained that the Bulgarian would not wear the bathrobe because it was red. Red was a Turkish color."

wards with as many as 50 beds and a nurse's station in the middle. When a patient's privacy was called for, a temporary screen was brought in. Even so, the hospital's patients—many of whom had never before slept in a real bed—thought the accommodations were luxurious. Inge Matthies Nastke, a German immigrant, marveled at the five weeks she spent in Ward 17: "The beds were good and we were given all the attention we needed and we were constantly being checked for fever and listened to our hearts. It was really being well cared for."[8]

Most patients remained in the hospital for a week or less. Diseases like measles and scarlet fever could be fatal, but patients ordinarily survived and were discharged once well enough to leave. Many of these patients were children. An attending physician wrote of going from bed to bed in the children's ward, dragging a reflecting light with which to check the throats of the several dozen youngsters bedded there.[9] Still other patients had medical problems that required remedial care. Dr. Bruce Anderson told of removing casts placed on patients before they sailed for America. "During a change of dressing on a thigh," wrote Dr. Anderson, "I pulled a piece of bone—almost an entire femur came out."[10]

Stubborn illness meant a longer hospital stay, provided the patient could pay for it. The fee was not particularly high—roughly two dollars a day. Nevertheless, it was beyond the means of many immigrants, who were often penniless when they arrived. The daily fee also exceeded the wage of a typical laborer. Unless a private charity or relative stepped forward to pay for patients' hospital care, they faced deportation, as was the case with Leie Kwarczinsky, a 30-year-old Russian immigrant. Her husband had arrived months earlier and was making $15 a week working 12 hours a day as a blacksmith on New York's subway construction project. When she arrived with the couple's children, ages 3, 7, and 9, doctors discovered she had trachoma. Her treatment continued into a fourth month without a cure, and her husband ran out of money at which point the commissioner of immigration on Ellis Island, Robert Watchorn, ordered her deportation. Watchorn noted that the woman's husband was unable to "make any further payments and . . . [Watchorn has] requested that deportation take place by the next available vessel." On Christmas Eve of 1908, Leie sailed for Russia aboard the *S.S. Scharnhorst*, leaving behind her husband and three children.[11]

Most immigrants with Class A conditions—those calling for deportation—did not receive hospital care because they could not afford it. Of those who applied for hospitalization, however, only one in eight was denied treatment by the medical staff.[12] Tens of thousands of patients were nursed to health at the Ellis Island Hospital and released to pursue their dream of citizenship.

Of the diseases treated regularly at the Ellis Island Hospital, none resisted cure more stubbornly or required more painful treatment than did trachoma. Today the disease can be treated with antibiotics administered orally. In the early 1900s, the procedure took weeks to complete without assurance of success. A cure required destroying the living tissue that harbored the trachoma bacilli, which could be accomplished by scarring the underside of the eyelid through periodic scraping with an abrasive stone and swabbing with a corrosive liquid.[13] It took three people to apply the treatment: a physician to abrade the eyelid and two muscular aides to hold the patient tightly in place. Josephine Gazieri, who was hospitalized for 11 months with trachoma, recalled the pain caused by the procedure: "Well, they used to use silver nitrate and blue stone. They used to rub the lids—turn the lids inside out, and burn . . . I had scars from the tears for at least five years . . . there was a chemical in there that would stain my face."[14]

If the trachoma procedure was more medieval than modern, the Ellis Island Hospital was otherwise a model of advanced medicine. Its diagnostic lab—equipped to identify rare diseases—was second to none. Its four operating rooms had the latest equipment, and the surgeons were highly skilled.[15] The hospital's work attracted the interest of medical doctors throughout the region. Autopsies were staged in the hospital's medical amphitheater before a packed gallery of visiting physicians, interns, and medical students.[16] Foreign physicians were also among those who flocked to Ellis Island to observe its medical practices. "Here to Study War on Tuberculosis" was how *The New York Times* on September 24, 1908, heralded the presence of a delegation of

"Believe it or not one of the ways of amusement at Island No. 2 where the General Hospital was located was to go swimming between Island 2 and 3." DR. GROVER KEMPF, U.S. PUBLIC HEALTH SERVICE

French physicians. Tubercular patients were housed in special infectious-disease wards and underwent a rigorous treatment regime: "Patients shall receive as much fresh air at all times as is practicable. Avoid drafts by using screens before windows. Patients without temperature must have a certain amount of exercise daily in the open air. . . ."[17]

Physicians at Ellis Island's General Hospital—one of three hospitals in the complex—felt their facility was unmatched by other general hospitals. Gleaming white iron beds lined the open wards and the mattresses were sterilized by the newly invented autoclave. Grover Kempf, a Public Health Service (PHS) physician at Ellis Island, claimed the facility "was like any general hospital, except it was done probably with better work than the ordinary general hospitals because of the number of graduate nurses and the number of doctors involved."[18]

Physicians at the Psychopathic

Pavilion—one of the two other Ellis Island hospitals—were even more convinced that their facility had few equals. It was here that pioneering mental testing procedures—some still in use today—were developed. One such test was based on the placement of pictures, blocks, and symbols, which mitigated the effect of language and education on test results. One of the test's originators, Dr. Eugene H. Mullan, said: "It is well in testing to use pictures that portray certain native scenes with which peasants are more or less familiar."[19]

Hall noted: "There is a special hospital on what is known as a third island, where all contagious diseases are sent, and, speaking generally, the appointments are all that can be desired for the treatment of the sick. The medical staff, including the doctors and the nurses, attendants and others number about one hundred and sixty. It is impossible to exaggerate the importance of the work done by the doctors at Ellis Island. I cannot describe it in detail in the narrow limits of this article, but it filled me with the same sort of admiration that I felt for the Army

{ THE WORK DONE BY THE DOCTORS AT ELLIS ISLAND FILLED ME WITH THE SAME SORT OF ADMIRATION THAT I FELT FOR THE ARMY CORPS OF ENGINEERS BUILDING THE PANAMA CANAL. }

The acknowledged jewel in the Ellis Island medical complex, however, was the Contagious Disease Hospital. Likely the finest of its kind worldwide, this unit's wards were spaced along a 500-foot-long central corridor and staffed by physicians skilled at treating everything from measles to typhus fever. Writing in *The Sunday World* after having observed activities on Ellis Island for two weeks, journalist Henry

Corps of Engineers building the Panama Canal; the admiration one naturally feels for a combination of sheer efficiency with unlimited devotion to duty."[20]

Old and young, often very poor, and rarely rich, the patients found solace in each other, even though they often did not share the same language. Josephine Gazieri described her trachoma treatment as "quite an education" and then noted: "I never saw an Italian all the time I was in Ellis Island. On the left of my bed there was Adoni Zoska was her name and she was around my age. We tried to communicate. She spoke only Polish and I spoke Italian. But youth has a way of finding the door open."[21]

Religious services and social programs were also sources of comfort. Sunday was marked by a Catholic Mass and a Protestant service, and a rabbi came each week to meet with Jewish patients. A library with books donated by the New York Public Library was located in Ward 32 on Island No. 3. By 1924 the library had nearly 5,000 volumes, about half in English with German publications accounting for the biggest share of the others. Many of the patients were illiterate. Even so, patients checked out 1,000 books and 200 periodicals a month.[22]

The social highlight for most patients was entertainment in the form of movies and variety shows, staged in the recreation rooms of the General and Contagious Disease hospitals. Singers, folk dancers, and theater artists—some brought in from New York City and some drawn from the ranks of the immigrant patients—enlivened an otherwise somber place.[23]

Social service workers for the Red Cross were a welcome sight at Ellis Island. They made daily rounds of the wards, helping patients make contact with relatives and giving them clothing and other small gifts. The Red Cross's annual report in 1915 listed the items distributed in that year alone: "1,000 toys, 500 picture books, 500 sticks of candy, 500 cakes of chocolate, about 363 garments, about 21 pairs of shoes, about 500 handkerchiefs, about 20 pounds of tobacco, about 2,000 post cards, 500 pencils, 500 cakes of soap, and 4 cases of illustrated magazines."[24]

The Red Cross ran the immigrant library and also an immigrant school on the island. An unknown number of children—those requiring extended care or whose parents were undergoing long-term treatment—began their English instruction at the Red Cross–run school. There, they also got lessons in American values. "It is surprisingly like other schools," said the Red Cross's Elizabeth Gardiner. "The Primary, Intermediary, and Advanced classes study hygiene and the three R's in English. Indirectly they learn neatness, good manners, and American ways."[25] Civic education was not confined to the school,

For children especially, the opening of the Contagious Diseases Hospital could mean the difference between life and death. The fatality rate for those with measles, a common childhood illness, dropped from a high of 30 percent to almost nothing. Still, separated from their parents, often unable to speak the language of their caretakers, many found the experience frightening.

"There were quite a number of babies involved and one became attached to them even if you couldn't speak their language! It was not necessary . . . to be able to speak a language to a child . . . all that was necessary was gentle and kind treatment." DR. GROVER KEMPF, U.S. PUBLIC HEALTH SERVICE, 1912

and children were not its only targets. Films produced by the U.S. government emphasized good hygiene, hard work, and civic virtue.[26]

Children were the most adaptive patients, bringing to the wards their special brand of mischief and wonder. Mothers were allowed to stay with sick infants, but children otherwise were left by themselves in the hospital. They found ways to turn the facility into a playground. "We were at the end of a hall, and we could see the Statue of Liberty," recalled John Henry Wilberding, who as a young boy was hospitalized with his brother after they arrived from Germany. "Well, with measles you're supposed to pull the curtain down. You know, the lights, they hurt your eyes. Well . . . there was a contest between the nurses and two little boys whether they were up or down."[27]

Wilberding, who would serve his new

"There are usually from six to twelve children in the Ellis Island Hospital. As a rule they are stunted in growth and bear traces of unwholesome nurture, but they pick up wonderfully under the skillful treatment of doctors and nurses, and the breezes from the beautiful harbor bring a tinge of color into their wan faces." THE NEW YORK TIMES, 1904

country honorably during World War II, also recalled the strange-tasting food that the hospital's kitchen provided. Some immigrants had never eaten white bread before, and others had never experienced anything *but* white bread. For the children, new foods were an adventure. Said Wilberding: "We had never had spaghetti before in our lives, and it had tomatoes on it. And it was new to us and strange. And it was on a tray and so we decided to hold the tray up and see how far it could

get to the edge before it slipped off. Well . . . one of them slipped off and it must have been mine because my brother jumped over the railing and he started helping me clean up. But an orderly was standing in the doorway. He had just dropped the food in and he was leaving, but he must have turned around when he saw that. But he didn't raise his voice, and he smiled—I think it tickled him a little—and changed the sheets."[28]

The Ellis Island Hospital was a life-giving place. Three hundred and fifty babies were born at the hospital and instantly became U.S. citizens. Some were named after the doctors and nurses who had cared for the mothers. For 3,500 patients, however, the Ellis Island Hospital marked the end of life's journey.[29] "Ellis Island was a place of great happiness and great sorrow," said PHS physician Bruce Anderson. "The coming together of families that had been separated for years was marvelous to see. Unfortunately, times did occur when a family had to be separated because of . . . death. Then, you wished you were someplace else."[30]

Ormond McDermott, the 19-year-old son of an Australian dentist, spent his final days at the Ellis Island Hospital.

Dec. 6th, 1920

Ir.Gustav Moberg

Funeral of Richard W. Moberg

To ERICSON & ERICSON, Dr.
UNDERTAKERS AND EMBALMERS

5 ATLANTIC AVE., BROOKLYN
BET. 3RD AND 4TH AVENUES
TELEPHONE 108 STERLING

157 EAST 22ND ST., NEW
NEAR THIRD AVENUE
TELEPHONE 2554 GRAME

Removing Remains from Ellis Island	$	15.00
Embalming		15.00
Casket		60.00
Outside box		12.00
Hearse to Grand Central Depot		15.00
Attendance		10.00
	$127	00

Rec'd Payment
Dec 6th 1920,
Ericson Ericson
By B. E. Hartig
Thank you

Traveling as a member of the steamship crew that brought him to America, he inadvertently left his passport on the ship and immigration officials refused to let him reboard to locate it. For nine days, McDermott was housed in the Ellis Island dormitories while his status as a temporary worker was investigated; he had planned to spend a year studying the "motor car" business at the Studebaker factory in South Bend, Indiana. During his stay in detention quarters with steerage-class passengers, he contracted scarlet fever and, despite being treated in intensive care, died on the sixth day of hospitalization. His parents refused to accept his death until his eldest sister opened his lead-lined coffin at the dock in Sydney. His father collapsed and his mother went into hysterics, from which she never fully recovered.[31] (See photos and captions on pages 114–117 for more information on the life and death of Ormond McDermott.)

Regulations governing contagious disease required that the body of a deceased patient be wrapped in a disinfectant-soaked sheet and sent to the morgue before it was released to an undertaker. No burials were permitted on Ellis Island, and the bodies of unclaimed or penniless immigrants were interred in paupers' graves on Hart Island or in unmarked graves in cemeteries such as Mount Olivet in Queens. Immigrants were occasionally laid to rest with no one in attendance save the undertaker and a priest, minister, or rabbi. Family members were usually in attendance, though. For those headed westward, it was often the only time they would stand at their loved one's grave site.

Invoice for the funeral of Richard W. Moberg, December 1920, one of 3,500 immigrants to die at Ellis Island Hospital.

"The coming together of families that had been separated for years was marvelous to see. Unfortunately, times did occur when a family had to be separated because of deportation or death. Then, you wished you were someplace else." DR. BRUCE ANDERSON, U.S. PUBLIC HEALTH SERVICE

Since burial was not permitted on Ellis Island, many immigrants were buried in paupers' graves in cemeteries around New York City.

"Received from the Chief Medical Officer, the following property of Edward Moran, age 55 years, admitted to the hospital, Feb. 14, 1928 and died in this institution Feb. 18, 1928: 1 hat, 1 pair shoes, 1 gray suit, 1 white shirt, 1 pair socks, 1 pair garters, 1 union suit, 1 belt, 1 overcoat, 1 pair gloves, 1 watch, keys, rosary beads, $23.15."

RECORD GROUP 85, IMMIGRATION AND
NATURALIZATION SERVICE RECORDS

Keys to 3 Doors in Ward 27-28 Area

D. A. R.
Occupational Therapy
U. S. MARINE HOSPITAL
ELLIS ISLAND, N. Y.

"The Public Health Service was a tightly knit group of men, many of whom were from the south, especially the University of Virginia, [and] most of whom were very able doctors. We as interns did the routine care." DR. BERNARD NOTES, U.S. PUBLIC HEALTH SERVICE, 1920

The medical staff at the Ellis Island Hospital had no choice but to act as jailers as well as caregivers. The hospital was both a detention center and a treatment facility. More than a few patients tried swimming to New York City, but no one is known to have succeeded.

"It cannot be denied that the sick or ailing immigrants receive very good care at the port of New York—very much better than they have ever experienced before in their lives. Some good folk, after a visit to the hospital, have permitted the rather natural suspicion to prey upon their minds that perhaps the immigrant was being better treated by the government than many disabled citizens of their own communities.

A GENERAL HOSPITAL FOR ALL NATIONS,
DR. MILTON FOSTER, U.S. PUBLIC HEALTH SERVICE, 1915

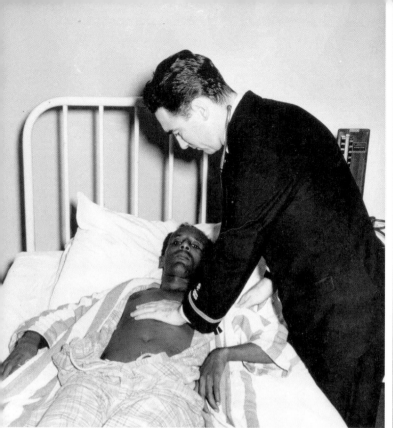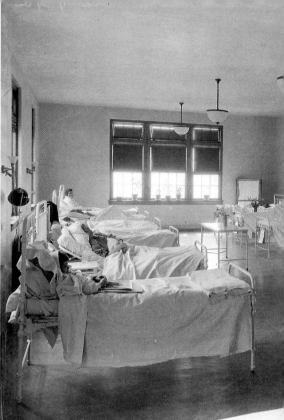

"Because the line was just routine inspection of an immigrant, in the hospital you were treating illness and you were a doctor there, I always felt. And I enjoyed it very much."

DR. GROVER KEMPF

88

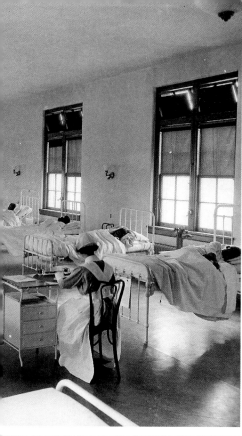

"I was in the children's ward. All those beds in a huge room and I tried so hard to ask, to find out, how long I would have to be there and what was wrong with me. I just wanted to talk and they couldn't understand me, they couldn't speak German, and I couldn't speak English."

INGE MATTHIES NASTKE, IMMIGRANT FROM GERMANY, 1912

"I have been in daily contact with the doctors and nurses and can testify to the kindness and care that the patients receive at their hands. It is not generally known perhaps that the hospital physicians and surgeons often call in specialists from the city in doubtful and obstinate cases."

REV. A. J. GROGRAN, ROMAN CATHOLIC CHAPLAIN AT ELLIS ISLAND, 1900–1923

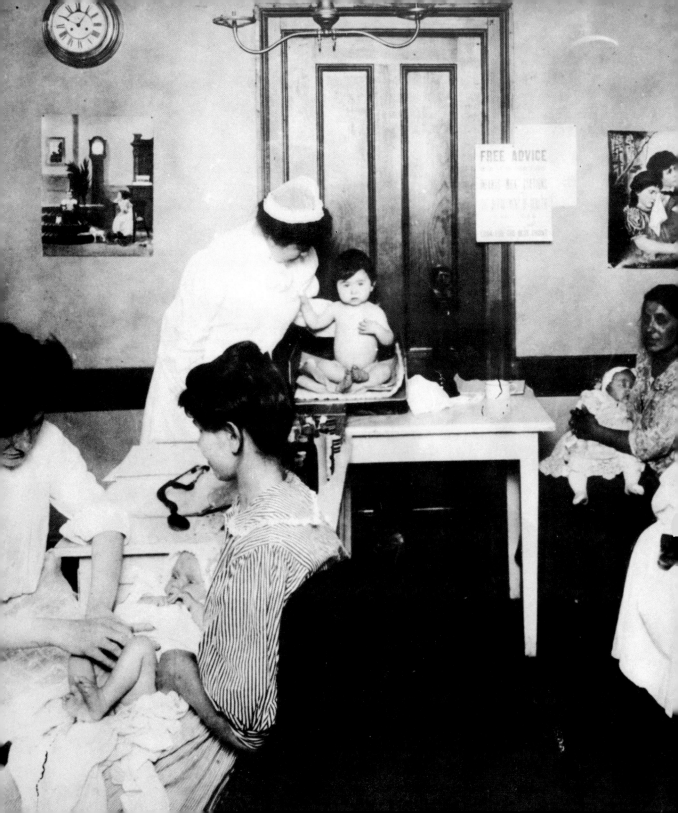

Public Health Service nurses, ward matrons, and Red Cross workers assisted immigrant mothers with caring for their babies as well teaching them about cleanliness, nutrition, and "good, American ways."

John Henry Wilberding and his brother, Ben, who were hospitalized with measles in 1928.

"When my stepfather came to Ellis Island to pick up four boys he could only take two because we were taken to the hospital."

A group of patients with favus, a fungal disease of the scalp. "After X-ray treatment a mild ointment such as Boric Acid is applied to prevent scattering of the hair. . . . Patient wears a protective bandage on the scalp during entire hospitalization."

DR. CARL RAMUS, ACTING CHIEF MEDICAL OFFICER

"They would rip all my hair out. Then they would put on a sweat cap with adhesive tape. Put it all around my head, and my sister's, and everybody in the ward. But then the day came when it was all cured." BESSIE COHEN AKAWIE, IMMIGRANT FROM UKRAINE WHO WAS HOSPITALIZED WITH FAVUS WHEN SHE WAS 11 YEARS OLD

"They looked at my throat and said that my throat was inflamed because I had my tonsils out in March and they thought I had diphtheria, or the beginnings of diphtheria, which was at epidemic stage at that time in New York. And I guess to play it safe they sent me to the hospital in isolation, or to quarantine." JOHN GAQUER, IMMIGRANT FROM FRANCE WHO WAS HOSPITALIZED IN 1929, WHEN HE WAS FIVE YEARS OLD

"They let me see my mother through double fencing where we couldn't touch, I would say maybe four feet apart. . . . It was very traumatic."

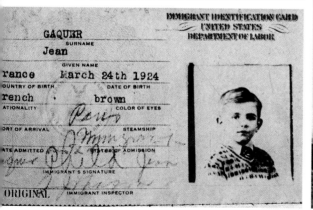

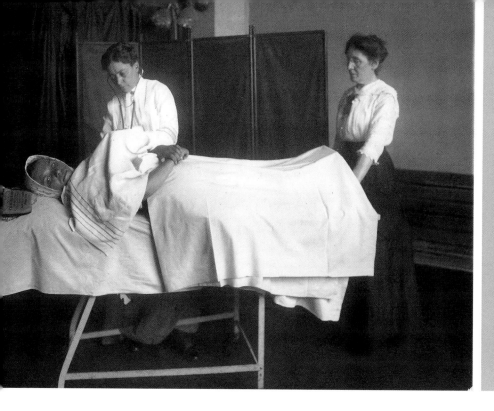

For many years, the Public Health Service doctors at Ellis Island were male, which presented a problem for the female immigrants—most of whom had never visited a doctor before the medical inspection and had never been touched by a man other than her husband. In 1913, Dr. Rose A. Bebb was hired as the first woman doctor at Ellis Island.

Medical staff of the Ellis Island Hospital, 1912.

"Quarters were provided on Islands No. 2 and 3 for medical officers, nurses, attendants, and orderlies. There were also quarters for other single employees but not married employees. The quarters were judged to be generally 'adequate' and 'sufficient.' One significant problem was that some of the quarters were located above the laundry which operated 24 hours a day." THE HISTORIC RESOURCE STUDY OF ELLIS ISLAND, VOL. II

One of four operating rooms at the Ellis Island Hospital.

"They operated on me. I don't think they gave me ether, because there was this big, bright light, and the room was full of nurses. Each one, they were holding my arms, they were holding my legs, and then the doctor was working on my ear. And I remember screaming, screaming. I must have passed out. That I remember. And when I came to, I was in the children's ward. I was there five weeks."

MARIA ALVARO NETO MARQUES, IMMIGRANT FROM PORTUGAL, 1920

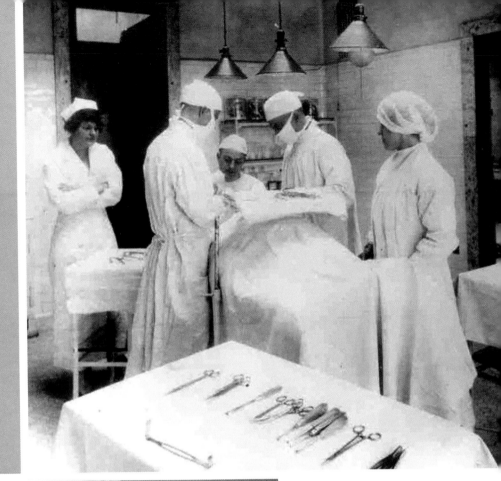

"Patient shall receive as much fresh air at all times as is practicable. Avoid drafts by using screens before windows. Patients without temperature must have a certain amount of exercise daily in the open air."

PUBLIC HEALTH SERVICE MEMO TO STAFF, 1922

Trachoma involved an inflammation of the eyelids that caused the eyelashes to turn inward, scraping the cornea and resulting in blindness. Today trachoma is treated with antibiotics, but in 1907 the best doctors could offer a patient was to scrub the inner eyelid (with a steel toothbrush) until a natural scar formed over the infection, gradually allowing the cornea to heal.

"Trachoma is a tedious disease, relapses are frequent, and at any time the disorder is likely to assume an intense inflammatory action. . . ." LETTER TO THE SURGEON GENERAL OF THE UNITED STATES, 1910

"Well, they used to use silver nitrate and blue stone. They used to rub the lids—turn the lids inside out, and burn. But when they did that, you had blue streaks running down your face, your mouth, your nose." JOSEPHINE GAZIERI CALLOWAY, IMMIGRANT FROM ITALY, 192

"We average about 1,000 circulations per month. From July 1, 1923, to March 1 the exact figures are 7,943, of which 2,692 are in English. You will see that our greatest need is for foreign books. The average mentality of our patients and their physical condition calls for light and interesting titles. Even a small amount of money received regularly would do a great deal to keep our book collection alive. The New York book dealers are interested in the library and have given us good prices. Several have sent us gifts of second hand books.

"It is a real hardship to tell members of the hospital force who are fond of reading, 'No, we have no new titles' and to the patients who have been confined to the hospital for several weeks, 'I am sorry, you have read everything in our collection.'" REPORT BY HELEN GRANNIS, CHIEF LIBRARIAN, ELLIS ISLAND HOSPITAL, 1924

Hospital patients in a locked porch of the Contagious
Disease Hospital.

"So far as the restriction of movement is concerned upon
the grounds surrounding the hospital, strict attention must
be devoted to the retention of patients." DR. EZRA KIMBALL SPRAGUE

Interior of a room in the Contagious Disease Hospital. Patients with tuberculosis were required to use two sinks to prevent the infection from spreading. When Leah Shain revisited the hospital seven decades after her aunt was deported from Ellis Island, she remembered the sadness people had often experienced there: "These buildings were filled with people who were desperate, whether from hunger or discrimination. . . . I feel these people all around me, all desperate to cross this little body of water as I know she wanted."

"They used to have . . . entertainers come through once in a while. . . . The one I remember, this guy came [and sang] "Pack Up Your Troubles in Your Old Kit Bag." I remember that part of it and it was kind of interesting. Every so often somebody could come out and entertain you. That's the only reason I learned English." EDWARD CHOLAKIAN, IMMIGRANT FROM ARMENIA, 1920

Christmas on Ellis Island.

"On the evening of December 24, the annual Christmas party was held in the Hospital Service room for all the patients in the hospital. About 300 patients and employees attended. The room was attractively decorated with holly and evergreen and a beautifully lighted Christmas tree stood beside the blazing log fire. An excellent quartet sang Christmas carols and the patients joined in the singing in their various tongues. Santa Claus made his appearance and distributed the brightly colored bags which were filled with gifts. Each small girl received a large doll, a toy, fruit, and candy. The boys received books, toys, fruit, and candy. The gifts to the women were beads, handkerchiefs, fruit, and candy. To the men were given neckties, handkerchiefs, fruit, and candy. Santa, accompanied by the choir, then proceeded through the hospital giving gifts to the patients, singing Christmas carols, bringing Christmas cheer to those whose journey to their new home in America had been interrupted by illness. Each ward in the hospital was decorated with a Christmas tree." THE RED CROSS NARRATIVE REPORT, 1924

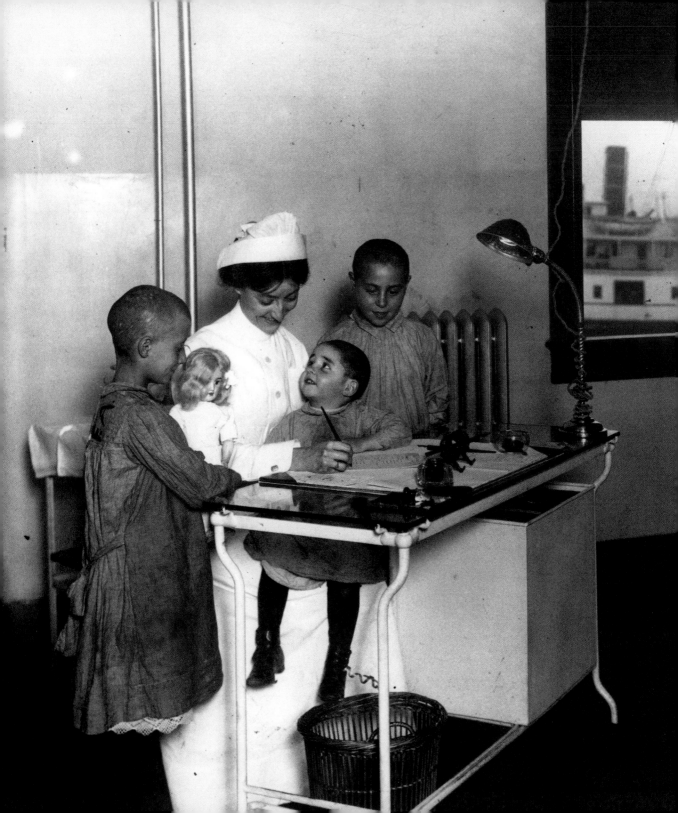

Children afflicted with favus, a fungal disease of the scalp and toenails.

"Miss Hannah, oh, she was so good. She was a nurse that you can dream about. She'd always bring me a present from New York City when she'd come. She would be off Sundays. I had a doll and I had some leather gloves and I kept them for many years." BESSIE COHEN AKAWIE, IMMIGRANT FROM UKRAINE, 1921

Board of National Missions
of the Presbyterian Church in the U.S.A.
156 Fifth Avenue, New York, N. Y.

MRS. MARY F. RIVERA, Representative
Social Service Room
Ellis Island, New York

DEPARTMENT OF
CITY, IMMIGRANT, AND INDUSTRIAL WORK

Ellis Island, Dec. 28, 1925.

Dear Mrs. Foxlee!

I received 148 packages of Christmas gifts exclusively, beside 27 boxes and 9 barrels of new and second hand clothing, during the month of December.

As Chairman of the Gift Committee, it was my priviledge to superintend the sorting and assembling of all gifts. As each apckage was received, its contents were assorted, so that when we began to prepare the bags for distribution, it was a simple matter.

The Hospital Social Service gave us a list of the aliens in the hospital, and we sent a corresponding bag for each alien, exactly like what was given on Island One. All gifts were placed in bags ready for distribution.

The Men's bags contained =
1 Tablet - 1 Pencil.
1 Pair Socks.
1 Game.
2 Handkerchiefs.
1 Necktie.
1 Towel.
1 Wash Rag, and 1 Soap.

The Women's bags contained -
1 Fitted Sewing Bag.
1 Bath Towel.
1 wash Rag - 1 Soap.
1 String of Beads.
2 Handkerchiefs.
1 Pencil.
1 Apron.
1 Pair of Stockings.

The Boy's bags contained -
1 Wash Rag - 1 Soap.
1 Game.
2 Handkerchiefs.
1 Pencil Box.
1 Necktie.
1 Harmonica.
1 Paint Box, and Picture Book.
1 Top.

The Girl's Bags contained -
1 Large Doll.
1 Smaller doll, dressed in 3 Handkerchiefs
1 Wash Rag - 1 Soap.
1 Box of Dishes.
1 Pair Stockings.
1 Rubber Ball.
1 Picture Book.
1 Box Crayons.

Respectfully submitted,

Mary F. Rivera

(Mrs.) Mary F. Rivera.

Children celebrate Christmas on Ellis Island.

"I opened the package and she [the nurse] had given me a little patent leather bag and two satin ribbons for my pigtails. And I was so happy and I, unfortunately, had never been able to speak to her, she didn't come to the ward again and I wanted to thank her because I really appreciated it and I wanted to tell her how happy it made me."

INGE MATTHIES NASTKE, IMMIGRANT FROM GERMANY, 1912

"And then they put me on a cart and I went down this long corridor and Mother was walking along beside me, with another nurse who had a hold of her arm. And the next thing I knew, when I turned around, my mother was no longer with me." ANN ELIZABETH NILSSON RIERSON, IMMIGRANT FROM SWEDEN WHO WAS HOSPITALIZED WHEN SHE WAS FIVE YEARS OLD

"I loved the food. I became very friendly with the cook. . . . I'd help her with washing. . . . We had potatoes, we had corn. [W]e had lettuce, but it was like pickled. [W]e thought that's the only way to eat lettuce, it would be in brine of vinegar and oil. But the thing we liked the best was the ice cream. . . ."

BESSIE COHEN AKAWIE, IMMIGRANT
FROM UKRAINE, 1921

The medical records of Ormond Joseph McDermott, who arrived on Ellis Island on February 16, 1921, from Sydney, Australia.

The eldest son of a prominent Sydney dentist, Ormond McDermott finished his Jesuit high school on the path to a career in sales, instead of attending university like his nine brothers and sisters. McDermott so impressed the American manager of the Studebaker Car Company who was visiting Sydney that Ormond agreed to spend a year in the South Bend, Indiana, factory learning the "motor car" business. McDermott was to be paid a small stipend, with his father subsidizing his living expenses.

On February 16, 1921, he arrived in New York Harbor on the ship Wandilla, having earned his ticket as a "workaway" member of the steamship crew. McDermott was dressed to the nines, wearing a suit, suspenders, and necktie with an overcoat; his shirt had cufflinks. At five feet six inches tall, Ormond Joseph, nicknamed "Little O.J." (his father being "Big O.J.") had sandy brown hair and blue eyes and was described by his niece as a "handsome lad."

But an act of forgetfulness, leaving his passport behind in his cabin, as well as his status as a temporary worker, aroused suspicion; immigration authorities ordered McDermott detained in the overcrowded dormitories on Ellis Island. For the next several days, the dapper salesman wandered among the "steerage" immigrants at Ellis Island, as he waited for authorization to land. But in the era before antibiotics, close quarters were risky for everyone; by the ninth day of detention Ormond had the telltale red rash signaling scarlet fever on his chest.

Because drugs did not exist to fight the infection, this highly contagious disease often led to heart failure and death. When Dr. W. H. Turner admitted McDermott to Ward 13 of the Contagious Disease Hospital, Ormond was running a fever of 102 degrees, with a pulse rate of 110. Public Health Service nurse Lucy Simpson swabbed his inflamed throat with liquid argyrols and gave him aspirin for the fever and pain. A doctor diagnosed McDermott as "rather acutely ill."

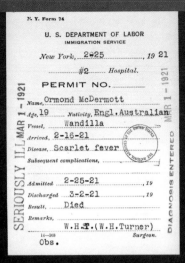

CLINICAL RECORD
BRIEF

Hospital U.S.Public Health Service Hospital #43,Ellis Island,N.Y.

Register No. 10036 Surname McDermott Given name Ormond

Permanent address

Name of nearest relative or friend With Immigration Service

Address of nearest relative " " "

Class of beneficiary Alien Compensation number ---

Former rank and organization ------

Age 19 Sex M Race W Married Single S Widower Divorced Religion Catholic

Nativity English-Australian Occupation ------

Source U.S.I.S.

Date of last service (in military service, on ship, etc.) -----

Authority U.S.I.S. Date and hour admitted 2/25/21--7:30PM

Condition on arrival Rather acutely ill Ward assigned 13

Remarks See physical chart

H.H.Richerson
Admitting Officer.

Diagnosis Scarlet fever *(Name)*

Number 1083 Date of diagnosis 2/26/21

Complication, change of diagnosis, sequela, intercurrent disease, etc. ---

Date of complication, etc. -----

Operation None

Date of operation ------

Where was condition incurred? Unknown When incurred? Unknown

How incurred? Unknown

Disposition Discharged

Condition on disposition Died Date of disposition 3/2/21

Autopsy: Yes-No. W.H.T.(W.H.Turner)
Ward Surgeon.

Name of Patient McDermott, Ormond Register No. 10036

Copy of Clinical Record.

U. S. PUBLIC HEALTH SERVICE

CLINICAL RECORD COVER

Over the next three days, Ormond slept fitfully, ate very little, and received medical treatments typical of the era: Brown's mixture and castor oil, camphor oil, Dover's powders and digitalis. On March 1, McDermott's temperature spiked to 105.2. "He is restless and wants to see his friend. Mind wandering," wrote his nurse. Ormond McDermott never had the chance to see this friend. Six days after being admitted to the hospital and less than three weeks after he arrived in America, he died early the next morning at 12:25 am.

Ormond's medical records are the only complete ones that remain from the Ellis Island Hospital era. National Park Service officials believe that the tens of thousands of other records have either been destroyed or are stored in an unknown federal facility. I located McDermott's records in immigration files of the National Archives in Washington, D.C. The files were located there because the McDermott family had requested, through the British government, to know the circumstances surrounding their son's death. The request landed on desk of the surgeon general, who ordered that McDermott's medical records be released to immigration authorities to "complete our showing that the boy had excellent care."

TREASURY DEPARTMENT
UNITED STATES
PUBLIC HEALTH SERVICE

OFFICE OF
MEDICAL OFFICER IN CHARGE

Ellis Island, N.Y.

March 8 1921.

RECEIVED FROM THE CHIEF MEDICAL OFFICER:

HOSPITAL NUMBER 10036:

Alein Ormond Mc Dermott, aged 19years, nativity, England, ex. SS. "Wandilla" February 16, 1921, placed in the U.S. Public Health Service Hospital February 25, 1921 died in that institution March 2, 1921.

Cause of Death Scarlet Fever.

- - - - - - - - - - - - - -

1 Coat 1 Pr Suspenders
1 Pr Trousers 1 Collar
1 Vest 1 Pr Shoes
1 Suit Underwear 1 Hat
1 Shirt 1 Overcoat
1 Necktie
1 British Passport

Studebaker Corp. of Amer.

H.C. Lackey
2 Rector St.,
New York.

..., the Governor-General of the
Commonwealth of Australia, request,
in the name of His Britannic
Majesty, all those whom it may
concern, to allow—

Ormond Joseph McDermott

to pass freely without let or hindrance,
and to afford him every assistance
and protection of which he may
stand in need.

Given at Government House
Melbourne in the State of
Victoria in the Commonwealth
of Australia, this 4 day of
June One thousand nine
hundred and Twenty One.

Forster.

Governor-General.

Age	19 years
Profession	Motor Car Salesman
Place & date of birth	Sydney, N.S.W.
Maiden name if widow, or married woman travelling singly	17th December 1901
Height	5 feet 6 inches
Forehead	Oblong
Eyes	Grey
Nose	Straight
Mouth	Small
Chin	Normal
Colour of Hair	Medium Fair
Complexion	Fair
Face	Small
Any special peculiarities	Mole near left eye
National Status	Natural Born British Subject

This passport is valid for two years only
from the date of its issue. It may be renewed for
four further periods of two years each after
which a new passport will be required.

RENEWALS.

1.

2.

PHOTOGRAPH OF BEARER.

SIGNATURE OF BEARER.

Ormond McDermott's family was located in Sydney by genealogists whom I enlisted for the task. Anne McDermott Keeling, the daughter of Ormond's brother, spoke about how Ormond's death had become a taboo chapter in their family history, for decades rarely spoken of. Ormond's parents suffered considerably upon learning that "Little O.J.," their first-born son, had died in the Ellis Island Hospital; his mother had a breakdown and for months his father was unable to work at his dental practice. For a time, relatives stepped in to help raise the large family. When Ormond's body was shipped back to Australia in a lead-lined coffin, his sister Estelle was there to meet it at the wharf. Ormond Joseph McDermott was the first person to be buried in the family plot at South Head Cemetery in Vaucluse, Australia.

CHAPTER 4

REJECTING THE "RIFF RAFF"

"... THE ADMISSION OF MENTALLY DEFECTIVE IMMIGRANTS STRIKES
AT THE VERY ROOT OF THE NATION'S EXISTENCE."[1]

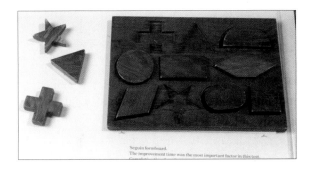

Seguin formboard.
The improvement time was the most important factor in this test.

*"Obviously the task of picking out from amongst this heterogeneous
mass those suffering from any mental disability is a gigantic one. . . .
Their general physical condition is often far from good
and their ignorance beyond belief."[2]*

WILLIAM WILLIAMS, ELLIS ISLAND
Commissioner of Immigration

the demand for labor was slowing, and the heavy concentration of immigrants in major cities strained the capacity of local schools. The crime-ridden slum neighborhoods that had sprung up in U.S. cities fueled a belief that the new arrivals were more of a curse than a blessing. For old-line Americans, the new arrivals' darker skin and suspect religious practices were bad enough. The thought that they might be ruining the country was altogether too much to accept.[3] A 1907 *New York Times* headline blared: "Immigrant Type Low, but 1,100,735 Get In: Quality Much Below Former Year, Says Commissioner."

The psychiatric hospital at Ellis Island became a place where assumptions about the new immigrants' inferiority intersected with medical ignorance to produce an ugly chapter in the hospital's history. U.S. law barred the entry of those considered "feebleminded," which became a device to keep "undesirables" out of the country.

Initially the Ellis Island medical complex had no special facility for those suspected of having mental illness. After two psychiatric patients committed suicide in the General Hospital in 1906, it was decided that a separate facility was needed.[4] When the Psychopathic Pavilion opened a year later, the two-story facility was a model of modernity. Like insane asylums of the period, it had locked wards and soundproofed walls, but unlike the others, it also had open, airy wards. The pavilion even had a veranda, though it was enclosed unlike other verandas in the hospital complex. Dr. Thomas Salmon, a Public Health Service (PHS) psychiatrist who helped design the facility, insisted that it resemble the other buildings of the complex. "Every suggestion of the cell-like rooms which used to be thought necessary in hospitals for the insane should be studiously avoided in the furnishing of this pavilion," said Dr. Salmon. "The duty to give these unfortunate persons the same degree of consideration that is shown to immigrants with other acute diseases is a very obvious one."[5]

The Psychopathic Pavilion differed from the other Ellis Island hospital units in a critical respect: it was not a place where immigrants could expect to be healed. Psychiatry was in its infancy as a medical specialty, and precise diagnoses of diseases like manic-depression and schizophrenia

were years away. Drug therapy and electroshock treatment had not yet been devised as ways to confront mental illness. Immigrants suspected of mental illness were sent to the Psychopathic Pavilion for further testing and, if diagnosed as feebleminded, held until they were deported.

In 1909, William Williams returned to Ellis Island for his second term as immigration commissioner, convinced that feebleminded arrivals were slipping past the medical inspectors. Like many other Americans, Williams believed mental illness was on the rise and that new arrivals were contributing to this trend. "A word as to the feebleminded," said Williams. "Not only are they likely to become a public charge on the community, but they are also quite likely to join the ranks of the criminal classes. In addition they may have feebleminded descendents. Many immigrant children who are feebleminded or mentally backward may be found in

Patients from the Ellis Island Psychopathic Pavilion awaiting deportation. During the great wave of immigration, psychiatry was in its infancy; only years later would psychotropic drugs and other therapies be developed to treat the mentally ill. Dr. Thomas Salmon, a Public Health Service physician who worked with the mentally ill at Ellis Island, noted: "Every effort is made to pick out those whose appearance even remotely suggests the existence of mental disease or the possession of a 'psychopathic organization.' If the manner seems unduly animated, apathetic, supercilious, or apprehensive or if the expression is vacant or abstracted the immigrant is held and carefully examined."

the public schools of our large eastern cities."[6]

"Now is the time," Williams continued, "to take greater precautions to differentiate between the good and the bad immigrant . . . this will be possible only when parasites who come here with no purpose of becoming productive forces shall be held back and they shall not fill up our congested cities." Williams believed feebleminded children were getting a free pass into the country. "Many children under five come here, and it is probably correct to say that nothing short of an inquiry into their heredity will enable the government to determine whether or not they are likely to grow up feebleminded," he said. "There are today in the public schools of New York many children of immigrants who are feebleminded or mentally backward, and one reason why

they passed our medical officers is that they arrived very young."[7]

The physicians on Ellis Island had no qualms about certifying immigrants as feebleminded. "The interests of this country," said Dr. Salmon, "demand an unremitting search for insane persons among the hundreds of thousands of immigrants who present themselves annually at our ports of entry."[8] But how were Ellis Island's physicians to identify the insane among the several thousand passengers coming through the medical line each day? These officials were trained to spot raging fevers and deformed bodies, not disturbed minds.

To tighten mental inspection standards, Williams persuaded the prominent psychologist Henry H. Goddard to take over that part of the admission process. Goddard was a follower of France's

After two suicides occurred at the General Hospital, the Psychopathic Pavilion (pictured here under construction) opened on the Island No. 2 in 1907. Along with the main facility were two oblong buildings capable of holding 50 people for observation and evaluation. For the most disturbed cases, there were small isolation rooms. Dr. Thomas Salmon wrote: "A psychopathic pavilion in connection with the present hospital would, then, fulfill three important purposes: 1) to provide adequate facilities for the observation of suspected cases of insanity; 2) to make it possible to give humane and efficient treatment to those immigrants who, during the voyage to America, become the victims of acute mental disorders—curing the curable and tiding the others over a distressing phase of their malady—and 3) to afford a suitable place for the temporary detention of those awaiting deportation. . . ."

Alfred Binet, who less than a decade earlier had devised a pioneering test of human intelligence. Goddard, formerly the head football coach at the University of Southern California, was the first to translate Binet's test into English and adapt it to mental health diagnosis, proposing that the terms "moron," "imbecile," and "idiot" be used to describe progressive levels of mental impairment.[9] Goddard implemented a two-step screening process for Ellis Island. New arrivals would first be questioned and observed by the medical inspectors, who would look for expressions or behaviors that might signal mental illness. As Dr. Thomas Salmon described it, "Every effort is made to pick out those whose appearance even remotely suggests the existence of mental disease or the possession of a 'psychopathic organization.' If the manner seems unduly animated, apathetic, supercilious, or apprehensive, or if the expression is vacant or abstracted, the immigrant is held."[10]

The second step was an intelligence test that Goddard administered to anyone suspected of feeblemindedness. Large numbers of them failed the test. Goddard found roughly 80 percent of Italian,

Jewish, and Russian immigrants to be mentally deficient, though he later cut that percentage in half.[11] Heralded in Congress and headlined in American newspapers, Goddard's findings fueled the claims of those seeking to stem the influx of southern and eastern Europeans into the country.

Goddard's work contributed to the study of eugenics—the notion that racial and ethnic groups differ in their intellectual capacity as a result of genetic differences. Shortly before beginning his tenure at Ellis Island, Goddard published *The Kallikak Family*, which traced a family through several generations and showed particular branches to have a high incidence of feeblemindedness. Mental testing on Ellis Island furthered Goddard's claim that intelligence was inherited.

Although Goddard had a scientific interest in genetics, his findings were seized upon by the politically minded. Dr. Rupert Blue, the Surgeon General of the United States and thereby head of the Public Health Service, was an unabashed eugenicist. He participated in eugenics organizations, wrote articles supporting their claims, and lavishly praised Madison Grant's *The Passing of the Great Race*

(1916), which argued that the American gene pool was being corrupted by recent immigrants and blacks.[12] Grant's claims on Nordic superiority were echoed less than a decade later in the writings of Adolf Hitler.

Whether Commissioner William Williams was a eugenicist is unclear, though he lambasted immigrants' physical, mental, and cultural fitness in a 1912 article, "Invasion of the Unfit." Wrote Williams:

ethnic groups on the basis of innate intelligence. Writing in *Popular Science Monthly* in 1913, Dr. J. G. Wilson claimed: "[T]he Jews are a highly inbred and psychopathically inclined race" whose defects are "almost entirely due to heredity."[14]

Immigrant aid societies protested Goddard's testing program, saying that stress, language barriers, and cultural

{ "IT IS THE DUTY OF THE OFFICERS OF THE PUBLIC HEALTH SERVICE AT ELLIS ISLAND TO SAFEGUARD THE COUNTRY AGAINST THE ADMISSION OF THESE LUMPS OF POISONOUS LEAVEN." }

"The admission of mentally defective immigrants strikes at the very roots of the nation's existence. It is from these and their descendents that the criminal classes are largely recruited; they crowd the insane asylums. . . . It is the duty of the officers of the Public Health Service at Ellis Island to safeguard the country against the admission of these lumps of poisonous leaven."[13]

Senior PHS physicians, including several at Ellis Island, were active in the eugenics movement and were less hesitant than Williams or Goddard to categorize

differences rendered it nearly worthless, a view shared by some PHS physicians. In a 1914 article in *The Survey*, a social policy journal, Dr. Ezra Kimball Sprague was quoted as saying that immigrants performed markedly better on intelligence tests after "a good night's rest combined with quiet and good food." However, the article claimed Sprague's views "were not widely shared by his colleagues" and that his remarks reflected "the moral dilemma of an honest officer who was reluctant to confer upon the immigrant a permanent stigma . . . and

President William Howard Taft visits Ellis Island in 1910, after reappointing William Williams (second from right) to his second term as commissioner of immigration. During Williams's four-year absence, immigration had spiked. President Taft prevailed on Williams as a fellow "Yale man" to enforce stricter immigration laws at Ellis Island, especially those targeting the "feebleminded" immigrant. During the course of Williams's second term, a record number of immigrants failed the mental examination and were deported.

possibly making him an outcast into some European port."[15]

But Sprague was not alone in challenging Goddard's testing program. Dr. L. L. Williams argued that no single mental test should determine an immigrant's fate. Writing in the *American Journal of Insanity* in 1914, Williams contended: "A certificate based on insufficient grounds means unnecessary and painful separation of families and the sending back of an alien to the ends of the earth regardless of the hardship involved. . . . In view of the serious consequences, as our findings are frequently combated at Ellis Island, at Washington, and in court, and as all of our work is thus done in an atmosphere of hostility, we cannot afford to depend upon any single test, no matter how valuable, or to adopt a mode of procedure which would result in mechanically grinding out a diagnosis."[16]

The common sense that some immigrants displayed during mental screening bolstered such claims. In one instance, when a woman was asked whether it was better to sweep a dirty staircase from top to bottom or bottom to top, she answered that she hadn't come to America to sweep stairs.[17] Another immigrant was given the problem of adding 2, 3, and 4 and was unable to do so. Then he was asked, "If you had two horses, three cows, and four sheep, how many animals would you have?" To which he replied, "Oh, if I were as rich as that, I would never have come to America."[18]

Goddard's test results were skewed by immigrants' impoverished backgrounds. Parochial in their thinking, many had little or no formal education. As Dr. Eugene H.

Mullan observed: "The farmer of southern Italy, tilling a few acres of land and living in a hut . . . can hardly be expected to define the word 'charity.' He has never been 50 miles from his place of birth. He could not go into a room in an ordinary American home and give the name in his own language for even a small part of the things he would see there, because he has never seen or heard them before."[19]

Mullan and some of his colleagues—most notably, Howard Knox—developed alternative methods to test immigrants' mental abilities. They employed blocks and symbols as a means of reducing the test effects of education and language. Their methods were used widely elsewhere in subsequent decades.[20]

Although the new tests made it easier for immigrants to pass the mental exam, eugenics and the deportations encouraged by the theory had become entrenched at Ellis Island. Hospital records include a request for "one set of anthropometric instruments, consisting of three metal calipers" to be used to measure the circumference of an immigrant's head, with the results sorted into racial and ethnic categories.[21] Demand for the findings

extended to the Smithsonian Institution. In a January 21, 1919, letter, the Smithsonian's curator of physical anthropology, Arles Hrdlicka, requested regular "anthropometric measuring," saying "the physical as well as the mental make-up of the future population of this country must be a composite shaped partly by the new environment, but in the main based on the hereditary qualities . . . brought into the country by the European immigration."[22] Seven years later, Hrdlicka, whose personal opinion of eugenics is not known, was still pursuing his research. Writing to the surgeon general on March 6, 1926, Hrdlicka noted: "These studies must soon show whether or not the fears of some of our eugenicists and recent writers as to the probable harm through further immigration to the American people are well founded."[23] Soon thereafter, however, interest in Ellis Island's anthropometric program waned because immigration had slowed to a trickle.

No record exists of the number of people wrongly deported from Ellis Island on the grounds that they were feebleminded. Surely hundreds fit this category, if not thousands.[24] The future New York mayor Fiorello La Guardia wrote in his memoir: "I always suffered greatly when I was assigned to interpret for mental cases in the Ellis Island Hospital. I felt then, and I feel the same today, that over fifty percent of the deportations for alleged mental disease were unjustified. Many of those classified as mental cases were so classified because of ignorance on the part of the immigrants or doctors and the inability of the doctors to understand the particular immigrant's norm or standard."[25]

The hardship imposed on immigrants and their families by deportation is beyond doubt. In 1924, 15-year-old Hildegard Hallgren was diagnosed as mentally deficient after having traveled to Ellis Island from Sweden with her family. Her sister, Linnea, recalled the ordeal: "We got through our tests and we were all ready to land. But they found fault with my sister . . . they said she had eye trouble . . . and then also from her crying and being so nervous all the time they declared that she was intellectually subnormal." Despite her family's appeal to immigration authorities, she was ordered to leave the country. Her father, brother, and Linnea left Ellis Island for their new home in Massachusetts, while the teenager and her mother took a steamship back to Sweden. "When we landed in Goteborg we were homeless," wrote Mrs. Hallgren in her diary. "We had sold our home and all possessions before we left for the U.S. We now live in hope that God will direct us so that our separation with our children in America will not be too long." But the years turned into decades, and the Hallgren family was never reunited. "Ellis Island has always been called the Island of Hope and the Island of Tears," Hallgren's sister said. "For my family it has been the Island of Tears, all of our lives."[26]

Hildegard Hallgren and her parents, 1943, outside the mental institution in Sweden where she lived until her death in 1973.

"All our lives Ellis Island was the Island of Tears, all of our lives, that's what it was to my family," said Linnea Hallgren.

"A young girl in her teens from the mountains of northern Italy turned up at Ellis Island. No one understood her particular dialect very well, and because of her hesitancy in replying to questions she did not understand, she was sent to the hospital for observation. I could imagine the effect on this girl who had always been carefully sheltered and never permitted to be in the company of a man alone, when a doctor suddenly rapped her on the knees, looked into her eyes, turned her on her back, and tickled her spine to ascertain her reflexes. The child rebelled—and how! It was the cruelest case I ever witnessed on the island. In two weeks' time that child was a raving maniac, although she had been sound and normal when she arrived at Ellis Island."

FIORELLO LA GUARDIA, *THE MAKING OF AN INSURGENT*, 1948

A woman takes an exam with Dr. Howard Knox, the creator of alternative mental tests for immigrants that depended less heavily on language proficiency for passage.

"Their general physical condition is often far from good and their ignorance beyond belief. Not only are many illiterate, but many do not know the days of the week, the months of the year, their ages, or any country in Europe outside of their own."

WILLIAM WILLIAMS,
COMMISSIONER OF IMMIGRATION, 1910

An editorial cartoon calling for a "finer screen" against the increasing numbers of immigrants coming from southern and eastern Europe.

"The duty to give these unfortunate persons the same degree of consideration that is shown to immigrants with other acute diseases is a very obvious one, for the cure of acute mental disease is as much a requirement of humanity as the cure of pneumonia or of typhoid fever. The deportation of those who recover would still be mandatory under the provision of the law excluding persons who have been insane within five years." DR. THOMAS SALMON, 1905

"Many immigrants come from rural districts where opportunities have been meager, they have departed from their relatives and friends, they have undergone a long voyage perhaps suffering many hardships, they are anxious to land and meet relatives. Hence, their mentality is in a condition which has been partly shaped by all of these circumstances."

THE NORMAL IMMIGRANT, DR. EUGENE H. MULLAN,

U.S. PUBLIC HEALTH SERVICE, 1917

"Should the immigrant appear stupid and inattentive to such an extent that a mental defect is suspected, an 'X' is made with chalk on his coat at the anterior aspect of his right shoulder. Should definite signs of mental disease be observed, a circled 'X' would be used instead of the plain 'X.' Dr. Eugene H. Mullan, "Mental Examination of Immigrants," Public Health Reports, 1917

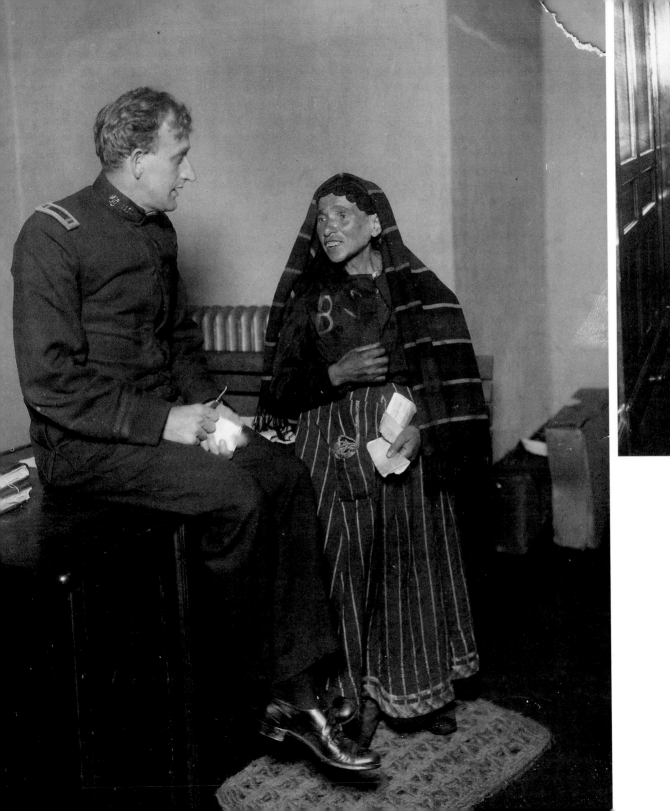

"The purpose of our mental measuring scale at Ellis Island is the sorting out of those immigrants who may, because of their mental make-up, become a burden to the State or who may produce offspring that will require extra care in prisons, asylums, or other institutions."

DR. HOWARD KNOX, *SCIENTIFIC AMERICAN*,
"MEASURING HUMAN INTELLIGENCE," 1915

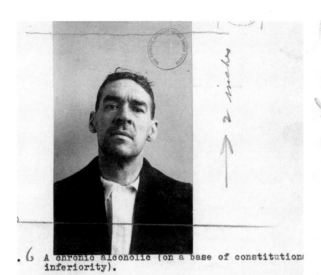

Fig. 6 A chronic alcoholic (on a base of constitutional inferiority).

Fig. 10 A typical expression of anxiety.

Fig. 4 Low moron. Age 30 years.

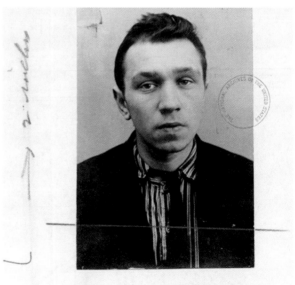

Fig. 8 Dementia precox. Apathy.

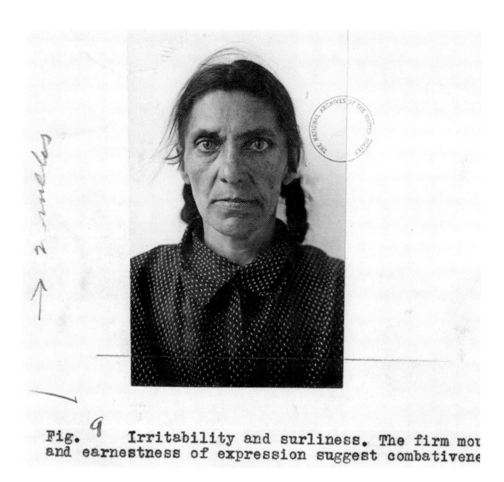

Fig. 9   Irritability and surliness. The firm mou
and earnestness of expression suggest combativene

Photographs of immigrants at Ellis Island who were pulled from the medical inspection line and given further mental tests.
"Individuals possessing dull, stupid, indifferent, and apathetic countenances devoid of expression should be investigated
more thoroughly for feeblemindedness." "A DIAGNOSTIC STUDY OF THE FACE," DR. HOWARD KNOX, U.S. PUBLIC HEALTH SERVICE, 1913

Fig. 11 Advanced juvenile paretic. Expression of
The facial expression suggested feeble-mi

"Insanity among immigrants is daily increasing. The matron in charge of the women's quarters on Ellis Island explains that homesickness and lack of knowledge of the English language are the chief causes of mind derangement among female aliens."

"REFUSED AN ENTRY TO THE PROMISED LAND,"
THE NEW YORK TIMES, 1906

Fig. 7 Dementia precox. Facial rigidty and clen teeth.

146

g. 14 Dementia paralytica. Expression earnest, attent and serious. Does not suggest mental disorder.

Well marked manic state, happy and overactive yet the expression does not suggest it. In fa *mental disorder of no kind is suggested.*

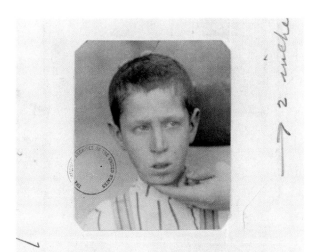

g. 2 Low grade imbecile. Age II years.

33 --- Low grade imbecile, age 11 years.

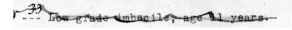

Fig. 13 An advanced paretic. Lack of tone and with ironing out of one naso-labial f

In 1929, doctors in the Ellis Island Psychopathic Pavilion received a letter from an Austrian psychiatrist offering them, for $100 each, a "maniac bed," something he had constructed specially and used for the restraint of patients in the Vienna Psychiatric Clinic. Thankfully, the doctors declined.

Immigration inspectors take "Bertillon" measurements, named after Alphonse Bertillon, the inventor of "anthropometrics," a process used to identify people according to their measurements. In practice, it was unreliable as a means of personal identification and was eventually replaced with fingerprinting.

149

CHAPTER 5

FALLING INTO
DISUSE AND DECAY

"EXAMINATION ON THE OTHER SIDE IS TEN THOUSAND
TIMES BETTER THAN REJECTION ON THIS SIDE."[1]

*"No one can stand at Ellis Island and see the physical and mental
wrecks who are stopped there . . . without becoming a firm believer
in restriction and admission of only the best."*[2]

DR. ALFRED C. REED,
POPULAR SCIENCE MONTHLY,
"Going through Ellis Island"

NINETEEN TWENTY-ONE MARKED BOTH THE PINNACLE FOR THE ELLIS ISLAND HOSPITAL AND A PRELUDE TO ITS DEMISE. THAT YEAR, THE HOSPITAL ADMITTED 16,666 PATIENTS—

the most of any year.[3] But 1921 was also the year that Congress began to limit immigration and, with that, to close the door on the hospital.

Immigration had slowed during World War I but rose sharply afterward as war refugees joined the ranks of those seeking entry. Americans were not in a welcoming mood, however. They were wary of eastern Europeans, having fought against Germany and the Austro-Hungarian Empire in the war and having read about the rise of communism in Russia. Distrust intensified when foreign-born anarchists detonated explosives in eight American cities, including a bomb placed on the doorstep of the home of Attorney General of the United States, A. Mitchell Palmer. The influenza pandemic of 1918–1919 heightened public anxiety even further. While the outbreak began in Europe, it eventually killed half a million Americans, many of them so young that the average life span in the United States fell by ten years.[4]

These developments infused the work at Ellis Island with urgency. Although nearly four dozen medical inspectors were now stationed at the facility, Congress had upped the list of conditions for excluding arrivals. Thirty-three categories now filled the list, including anarchists, assassins, and those opposed to private property, an expansive category that included communists, utopians, radical socialists, and others. Eliot Wadsworth, assistant to the secretary of the treasury, expressed the government's determination to expand the restrictions. "The least that can be done as a protection [of the country]," he wrote, "is to make absolutely sure that those who are mentally or physically unfit are stopped at the gateways and turned back."[5]

The inspection line slowed to a crawl as immigration officials sought to identify anyone who might be barred from entry. At times, as many as 15,000 immigrants were held on ships in New York Harbor, waiting their turn to land. Nevertheless, officials managed to process 560,000 arrivals in 1921, an average of 1,500 immigrants a day.[6]

Periodic outbreaks of dangerous disease helped Public Health Service (PHS) physicians to see themselves as something more than guardians of the gate. A typhus scare in 1921 put the hospital complex on alert for months. In one of the temporary detention rooms, an immigrant became seriously ill and was sent to the Contagious Disease Hospital, where a Felix-Weil test

indicated typhus. By the third day, his body bore the signature rash of the disease. Death came on the fifth day. For several days before falling seriously ill, he had been in detention with scores of other immigrants and they were shipped to the quarantine station at nearby Hoffman Island. The source of the typhus was never found, nor did other cases arise. Nonetheless, a typhus alert was in effect through the rest of the summer and the fall and continued into the winter and the next spring when a typhus outbreak occurred in Europe.[7]

In 1921, President Warren G. Harding signed a law imposing quotas on the number of immigrants that a country could send to the United States in a year—the figure was limited to 3 percent of its countrymen already living in the States. Enacted by overwhelming majorities in the House and Senate, the Temporary Quota Act was widely praised. James J. Davis, the secretary of labor, later a U.S. senator, and author of a book titled Selective Immigration (1925), claimed that "the regulation of immigration is about the most

In 1901, Captain John Halpin was smuggling immigrants off Ellis Island at night aboard the Samoset, *charging 50 cents a head. Although investigated and punished, Halpin continued to work as a government employee until 1910.*

important [issue]" facing the country.[8] Davis was himself an immigrant, having arrived from Wales with his parents at the age of eight.

The 1921 legislation was not the first effort by Congress to restrict immigration. In 1882, it had passed the Chinese Exclusion Act. Chinese laborers, known as "coolies," had helped build the West's railroads and dig its gold and silver mines. But as the need for their labor declined,

The 1921 Quota Act failed to satisfy those who wanted to stop altogether the influx of southern and eastern Europeans into the country. In 1924, Congress enacted the National Origins Act, which further reduced the level of immigration while using the 1890 census—the last one taken before the great wave of eastern and southern Europeans—as the basis for determining each country's quota. The effect was to ease the path of immigrants

{ THE SURVIVORS [OF THE *TITANIC*] WERE TRANSPORTED TO ELLIS ISLAND AND ALLOWED TO DISEMBARK—ALL EXCEPT SIX CHINESE SEAMEN. . . }

racial prejudice prompted Congress to bar all but a small number from entry. The 1882 law primarily affected the West Coast ports, but the sinking of the *Titanic* in the north Atlantic brought Ellis Island squarely into the picture. The survivors were transported to Ellis Island and allowed to disembark—all except six Chinese seamen, who received medical attention on board the rescue ship before being transferred to the British steamship *Annetta* and sent back to sea.[9]

from countries like England, Sweden, and Germany while creating a barrier to those from countries like Italy, Poland, and Hungary. Moreover, because the quotas were based on white Americans only, Asians and Africans were effectively barred from entry, with a token 100 immigrants a year allowed to enter from those countries. Speaking at the Statue of Liberty that same year, President Calvin Coolidge said without a hint of irony: "Those who do not want to be partakers of the American spirit ought not to settle in America."[10]

Among the witnesses invited to appear before Congress on the need for a new quota system was Henry Laughlin, an Anglo-Saxon supremacist and co-founder of the Eugenics Society. He testified as to the inferiority of certain racial and ethnic groups. "We in this country have been so imbued with the idea of democracy, or the equality of all men," said Laughlin, "that we have left out of consideration the matter of blood or natural-born hereditary mental and moral differences."[11]

A bubonic plague scare in 1924 strengthened lawmakers' determination to curb the flow of immigrants, while putting the PHS doctors at Ellis Island on high alert. "Public Health Service Prepares to Meet Increased Danger at Our Ports," blared a *New York Times* headline of December 20, 1924. The plague had already struck several Mediterranean ports, and passengers arriving from affected locations were quarantined.[12]

Bubonic plague did not infiltrate the United States in the 1920s, maintaining the Ellis Island medical facility's record as a place where disease was stopped before it

THE ONLY WAY TO HANDLE IT.

Editorial cartoon illustrating the effects of the quota laws on immigration.

reached the American mainland. No major epidemic was ever traced to an immigrant treated at the Ellis Island Hospital before entering the United States.[13]

With the flow of immigrants receding, the Ellis Island Hospital trimmed its operations, a process that quickened when health screening was shifted to U.S. consulates overseas. Immigrants would undergo a rigorous physical exam before being allowed to board ship for

America. Dr. John Thill, a PHS physician, described the change: "About the time that I completed my internship, another program was being instituted where the Public Health Service doctors would go to the various ports of entry over the world to examine these people, so that they would be spared the expense of spending their life savings to come to this country and being sent back."[14]

The new policy dictated that immigrants not be allowed to land at Ellis Island unless they had passport or visa problems or became sick en route. Several thousand immigrants each year still entered through Ellis Island, but this was a far cry from the thousands per day who had come in peak years.[15] And as the flow of immigrants slowed, the PHS further reduced its presence on the island.

Barely three decades after opening, the Ellis Island Hospital was fading. Its hallmark, the unrivaled Contagious Disease Hospital, sat practically empty.

At one point, the FBI opened an office in the medical complex to facilitate the deportation of suspected subversives. During World War II, disabled American servicemen were housed on the island, as were German and Italian prisoners of war. They were treated at the General Hospital, which in 1951 finally closed its doors. The complex's last occupant, the U.S. Coast Guard, shut down its operation in 1954, and the facility was left to decay.

Over the next half century, rain and salt air would pour through broken windows and leaky roofs, vines and trees would take root inside the buildings, and gulls and pigeons would nest in the rafters. In closing the facility, the government did not bother to empty it. Huge soup tureens sat with their tops askew in the hospital kitchen, while beds and gurneys were left to rust in the hospital wards. With time, fewer and fewer New Yorkers would know what the stately buildings in their harbor had once meant to America.

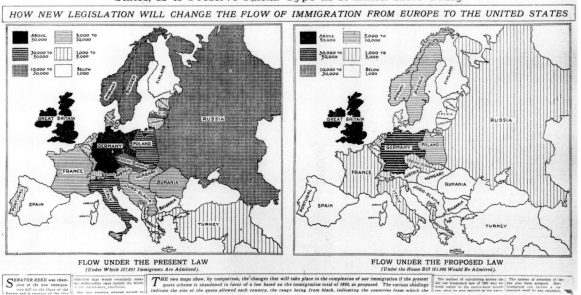

From The New York Times, *April 1924, one month before President Calvin Coolidge signed into law the Immigration Act of 1924, also called the National Origins Act. The law set quotas on the numbers of people who could immigrate to America.*

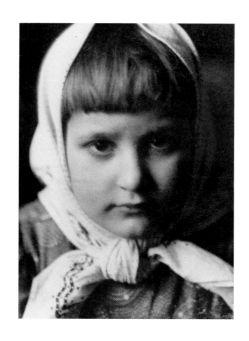

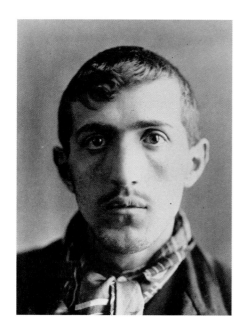

Thomas Allan, an immigrant from Scotland and a patient at the hospital in 1927, finds his former room during a visit in 2003.

"I was madder than hell because I kept telling them that I've already had chicken pox and I don't need to be quarantined and they said, 'Shut up, kid.' And we were in a ward over here. . . . It was 12 beds down one side and 12 down the other. . . . I spent my days jumping from bed to bed, madder than hell at America."

John Henry Wilberding and his wife, Ella. Seventy years after being treated for measles, John Henry remembered the kindness shown to him in the hospital. "To those who went through it, it was one of the most precious gifts you were given because when you were sick, you couldn't do anything about it. But here is a place that rescued you. That made you feel good that you were still being cared for and in a strange place thousands of miles away [from home]. People can never say that America isn't a place of compassion and understanding, because they certainly proved it there."

EPILOGUE:
IMAGES OF THE WAY IT WAS

RESTORATION OF THE ELLIS ISLAND HOSPITAL HAS BEGUN. IN 2000, CONGRESS GAVE THE NATIONAL PARK SERVICE A GRANT OF $11 MILLION TO STABILIZE THE BUILDINGS. THE PARK SERVICE has partnered with the nonprofit organization Save Ellis Island, which is raising the funds required to restore the site. The Save Ellis Island organization has worked closely with the New York Landmarks Conservancy and other organizations to develop the project, which is one of America's largest historic preservation efforts. Once finished, the National Park Service site will include an institute dedicated to the study of immigration—its effect on nations, cultures, economies, and public health. The Ellis Island Institute will include a conference center for hosting conventions, exhibits, and other public programs.

This effort is occurring two decades after restoration of Ellis Island's Great Hall began under the leadership of business executive Lee Iacocca. At the start of the Great Hall project, the photographer Christopher Barnes was hired to chronicle the restoration process. While doing so, the south side of Ellis Island, where the hospital stood, caught his eye. Over the next several years, he spent hours upon hours photographing the decaying buildings. The color photos in this book are from his collection. These photos, like those from the early 1900s when the hospital was open, are part of the historical legacy of this great American institution. Reflecting on his photographic work, Christopher Barnes observed:

I first became aware of, and intrigued by, Ellis Island through the timeless portraits created there by photographer Lewis Hine in the early 1900s. Every visage he captured reflected a story of human aspiration and social evolution.

In 1985 when I was hired to document the restoration of the Great Hall, I was thrilled to follow in the footsteps of many great photographers. Upon visiting the island for the first time, I was immediately drawn to the forgotten south side. The hospital, contagious disease wards, staff quarters, and other buildings had been virtually untouched for close to thirty years and were imbued with the resonance of lives and times past. Amazingly free of vandalism, the buildings were in what seemed to me a perfect state of decay, evocative and quite beautiful. As a photographer I considered myself very lucky to be able to explore and capture these spaces while they still emanated the spirit of the individuals who had long ago lived, worked, passed through, or possibly died there. I was afforded a brief window of time before the myriad of visitors, workmen, and other photographers that followed over the next five years would change these spaces forever.

ACKNOWLEDGMENTS

The research for this project was funded by three grants from the National Endowment for the Humanities (NEH). During the development of the funding proposals, David Weinstein, the NEH senior program officer, insisted that while the larger immigration issue would be important to the story, the hospital and the human story within its walls would distinguish this narrative from others. He repeatedly asked: "Why was the hospital built? Why was it important? What did it say about early twentieth-century America?" I am deeply grateful for his guidance and for the NEH's long-standing support for the project.

For one year, before restoration efforts began on the hospital buildings, the National Park Service gave my production company exclusive access to film the location for the production of a documentary film, which is a companion to this book. Cynthia Garrett, superintendent at the site of Ellis Island, and Frank Mills, deputy superintendent, were wonderful and supportive facilitators. So, too, were Don Fiorino and Dorothy Stroud, who were always willing to go out of their way in assisting my efforts. Without the cooperation of the National Park Service, I would not have been able to tell this extraordinary story. As challenging as the project has been, it was an opportunity like no other and I am deeply grateful for everyone's support.

Because no book had been written about the Ellis Island immigrant hospital, my research took me into case files, memos, personal writings as well as scrapbooks, policy statements, and other primary materials located in the National Archives and other institutions. Fascinating as these materials were on their own, they were like pieces of a jigsaw puzzle. In order to fit them together, I relied on a team of advisors, an NEH requirement that was a godsend. No author could have wished for a more talented and willing group than mine. Barry Moreno, the Ellis Island librarian and author of *The Encyclopedia of Ellis Island*, reviewed the manuscript and answered my endless questions patiently and thoughtfully. Alan Kraut, immigration scholar and professor of history at American University, contributed greatly to my effort to tell accurately "one of the last, untold chapters" in Ellis Island's history. His belief in my ability to develop the story, even when it seemed beyond reach, helped me keep going. A lifelong Yankees fan, Alan's e-mail to me after my beloved Red Sox finally won the World Series went something like this: "If Boston can win the World Series, you can produce this story." Fitzhugh Mullan, a third-generation Public Health Service physician whose grandfather was on the Ellis Island Hospital's medical staff, carefully read and corrected early drafts of my writing. Dr. Mullan also generously allowed me, in the preparation of this book, to use photographs and other materials belonging to his grandfather, Dr. Eugene H. Mullan. Howard Markel, pediatrician and medical historian at the University of Michigan, never failed to answer my "out of the blue" emails. His passion for the history of immigration and disease inspired and informed my research into the Ellis Island Hospital's history. John Parascadola, former historian for the Public Health Service, was enthusiastic about this project from the beginning and helped me get it off the ground. I also wish to thank Marian Smith, Alexandra Lord, and D'Arcy Hartman for their reviews of early drafts of the story.

Harlan Unrau's three-volume *Historic Resource Study*, published by the National Park Service, provided an institutional history of the workings of the hospital and of Ellis Island generally. The Ellis Island Oral History Project enabled me to listen to the voices and stories of the hospital's former patients, doctors, and ward matrons.

My production "team" was another invaluable resource. Several years ago, I was introduced to filmmaker Amy Stechler, whose immediate interest in this project provided strength and encouragement at a time when I needed it. The insights and suggestions of this valued friend and colleague helped clarify the story line I wanted to follow. Nancy Porter's expertise with historical documentary was helpful in determining ways to use the primary source materials found throughout the film and book. Marji Schmidt has been a loyal supporter and assistant on the project for many years. I appreciate her commitment and time in helping to make the book and film a reality. I have also benefited from membership in the Filmmakers Collaborative. Executive Director Bonnie Waltch and all of the talented producers in the group have offered support and expertise throughout the project.

When I received an answer to the e-mail I sent to the family of Ormond McDermott, a 19-year-old who died of scarlet fever at the Ellis Island Hospital in 1921, this narrative deepened on many levels. Learning from the family about the life and death of this young man, whose medical records I had found five years before in the National Archives, suddenly put a human face on a statistic—Ormond was one of 3,500 patients who never made it farther than Ellis Island. As I came to learn, Ormond's death became a forbidden topic of discussion among family members; I am most grateful for their help in gathering photos and information. I also wish to thank the following former patients: John Henry Wilberding, John Gaquer, Linnea Hallgren, Leah Shain, Tom Allan, and Anne Rierson, all of whom shared their memories of the hospital during videotaped interviews. These personal stories made all the difference, and I am most grateful for their efforts.

Ellis Island support staff such as George Tselos, Fran Desiante, Barbara Tate, Diana Pardue, Jeffrey Dosik, Alecia Barbour, Kevin Daley, Eric Byron, Judy Giuriceo, Janet Levine, Doug Tarr, and Vincent DiPetro helped facilitate countless days of research and filming.

I also wish to thank my book agent, Nancy Love, for helping me develop a successful book proposal and facilitating the contract with Smithsonian Books.

In addition to a cadre of professional advisors, I am blessed with a family and group of friends who supported this project through thick and thin. They know who they are, and I hold their love dear.

When the editorial team from Smithsonian Books toured the abandoned Ellis Island Hospital site last summer, they quickly grasped the importance of telling Ellis Island's "forgotten chapter." Elisabeth Dyssegaard, my editor, offered encouragement and advice to a producer who suddenly found herself in the role of author. Elisabeth's guidance was deeply appreciated. So, too, was the effort made by the production and design team. Shubhani Sarkar, Diane Aronson, Karen Lumley, and Judy Abbate created such a compelling layout, the photos tell their own story and truly enhance the book's narrative. Editorial assistant Dan Crissman helped me discover that book publishing is not all that different from film producing.

Lastly, I extend my heartfelt thanks and love to my husband, Tom Patterson, a remarkable scholar who never wavered in his support as I struggled to tell this story. Through his knowledge of American politics and history, I came to understand an era and the role it played in our nation's immigration history. Faced with reams of material culled from research trips and interviews, Tom helped me piece the giant puzzle together, urging me to bring the manuscript to a level I could only have imagined when the project began eight years ago. "Some things are worth the pursuit," he wrote to me at the outset. Little did we know then how long it would take to complete. But that never mattered to Tom, and for that I am profoundly grateful.

ILLUSTRATION CREDITS

Pages 1, 28, 63, 66, 71, 82, 96, 99, 110, 151: National Park Service, Statue of Liberty N.M./Ellis Island. Pages 37, 108, 134, 141, 192: Culver Pictures. Pages i, 8, 10, 11, 12, 18, 19, 20, 22, 47, 54, 70, 77, 80, 81, 90, 94, 100, 101, 102, 103, 112, 114, 118, 122, 142, 143, 144, 145, 146, 147, 149, 150, 191,: U.S. National Archives. Pages vi, 30, 35, 52, 74, 89, 104: Courtesy of the Department of Health and Human Services. Pages iv, 1: American Missionary Association Archives, Amistad Research Center at Tulane University. Pages 1, 16, 40, 42, 48, 53, 67 155, 186: Library of Congress. Pages 14, 46, 56, 87, 88, 97, 130, 132, 140: Brown Brothers, Sterling, PA. Pages 24, 25, 27, 50, 61, 126, 135: William Williams Papers, Manuscripts and Archives Division, the New York Public Library, Astor, Lenox and Tilden Foundations. Pages 26, 136, 158, 159, 160, 161: Watchorn Methodist Church Collection R. J. Milward curator. Page 31:

courtesy, Mütter Museum, the College of Physicians of Philadelphia. Page 44: Frederick Lewis. Pages 45, 148, J. H.Adams, Social Museums Collection, Harvard University Art Museums, 3.2002.2393, 13.2002.285.2 Pages 58, 106: State Historical Society of Wisconsin/University of Wisconsin. Page 60: from the archives of the YIVO Institute for Jewish Research, New York. Pages 62, 109, 119: Thomas B. Carcieri & Sons. Pages 64, 65: La Guardia Wagner Archives. Pages 68, 84: Museum of the City of New York.

Page 91: The Granger Collection, New York. Pages 92, 164: Thomas A. Wilberding & John H. Wilberding. Page 95: the Family of John Gaquer. Page 105: Boston Film & Video Productions. Pages 116, 117: McDermott-Keeling Family. Page 128: Courtesy of the Nephew of Linnea Hallgren. Page 157: © 2007 by the New York Times Co.; reprinted with permission. Page 162: The Allan Family.

NOTES

CHAPTER 1

[1]T. V. Powderly, 1902, "Immigration's Menace to the National Health," *North American Review*, 53–60, cited in Alan Kraut, *Silent Travelers: Germs, Genes and American Efficiency, 1890–1924*, Baltimore and London: The Johns Hopkins University Press, 58.

[2]Howard Markel, 1997, *Quarantine! East European Jewish Immigrants and the Epidemics of 1892*. Baltimore, Md.: The Johns Hopkins University Press, 93.

[3]"Outbreak of Cholera and Quarantine at New York Harbor 1892," *Harpers Weekly Journal of Civilization*, September 17, 1892. Information on Dr. Jenkins's instructions appeared in a front-page *New York Times* story, September 4, 1892.

[4]E. L. Godkin, 1892, "A Month in Quarantine," *North American Review* 155, no. 432: 737–744.

[5]William Williams Papers, New York Public Library.

[6]John Higham, 1955, *Strangers in the Land: Patterns of American Nativism, 1860–1924*, New Brunswick, N.J.: Rutgers University Press, 101. Also see Markel, *Quarantine!*, 166–182.

[7]*The New York Times*, August 29, 1892, cited in Howard Markel, 1997, *Quarantine!*, 88.

[8]Congressional debate on immigration restriction, 1921.

[9]James Davenport Whelpley, 1906, "The Open Door for Immigrants," *Harper's Weekly* L, no. 2573 (April 14): 517–519.

[10]The Spectator, 1907, *Outlook Magazine*, Ellis Island Library, box 21, Medical Inspection.

[11]Records of the Public Health Service, National Archives, Record Group (RG) 90.

[12]William Williams Papers, New York Public Library.

[13]Ibid. In 1917, Congress expanded the legal definition of "likely to become a public charge" to include "all idiots, imbeciles, feebleminded persons, epileptics, insane persons . . . persons of constitutional psychopathic inferiority . . ."

[14]Ibid.

[15]Letter from V. H. Metcalf, Department of Commerce and Labor, to William H. Taft, secretary of war, March 17, 1905, General Immigration Files, National Archives, RG 90.

[16]Letter from the Public Health and Marine Hospital Service to the Surgeon General, November 1902.

[17]Annual Report of the Commissioner General of Immigration, 1903, pp. 68, 71, General Immigration Files, National Archives, RG 85.

[18]Alfred C. Reed, 1913, "Going Through Ellis Island," *Popular Science Monthly* LXXXII, 11.

[19]U.S. Public Health Service Handbook for the Medical Inspection of Aliens, 1903.

[20]Annual Report of the Surgeon General of the Public Health and Marine-Hospital Service of the United States, 1905, 271–278.

[21]"Robert Watchorn," 1905, *Outlook Magazine*, cited in Harlan Unrau, 1984, *Historic Resource Study*, vol. 11, New York: National Park Service, 239–243.

[22]Ibid, 639–649.

[23]Ibid.

[24]Ibid.

[25]Harry F. Dowling, 1982, *City Hospitals*, Cambridge, Mass.: Harvard University Press, 32–33.

[26]Milton Foster, 1915, "A General Hospital for All Nations," *The Survey* (February), Ellis Island Library.

[27]Sir A. C. Geddes, 1923, "Dispatch from H.M. Ambassador at Washington Reporting on Conditions at Ellis Island Immigration Station," cited in Unrau, *Historic Resource Study*, vol. 11, 569.

CHAPTER 2

[1]Alfred C. Reed, 1912, "The Medical Side of Immigration," *Popular Science Monthly* LXXX: 384–390.

[2]Medical Certificate of Theodore Kelsch, August 14, 1908, General Immigration Files, National Archives, RG 85.

[3]Dr. Allan McLaughlin, 1905, "How Immigrants Are Inspected," *Popular Science Monthly* LXVI: 357–359.

[4]Amy L. Fairchild, 2003, *Science at the Borders: Immigrant Medical Inspection and the Shaping of the Modern Industrial Labor Force*, Baltimore and London: The Johns Hopkins University Press, 88.

[5]Dr. Grover Kempf, Oral History interview conducted in 1977 and covering his Public Health Service experiences at Ellis Island in 1912.

[6]Dr. Victor Safford, 1925, *Immigration Problems, Personal Experiences of an Official*, New York: Dodd, Mead, and Company, 249.

[7]Frederick J. Haskin, 1913, *The Immigrant: An Asset and a Liability*, New York: Fleming H. Revell Company, 27–34.

[8]Broughton Brandenburg, 1904, *Imported Americans*, New York: Frederick A. Stokes Company, 215–218.

[9]See Fairchild, *Science at the Borders*, 7.

[10]Dr. Milton H. Foster, 1915, "A General Hospital for All Nations," Records of the Public Health Service, 1912–1968, National Archives, RG 90.

[11]John Gaquer, 1999, videotaped interview at the site of Ellis Island Hospital.

[12]Leah Shain, 1999, niece of Pearl Yablonski, videotaped interview at the site of Ellis Island Hospital.

[13]William Williams Papers, New York Public Library.

[14]Letter to the Surgeon General, July 5, 1916, from Dr. Charles Lavinder.

[15]T. V. Powderly, 1902, "Immigration's Menace to the National Health," *North American Review*, 53–60.

[16]Thomas M. Pitkin, 1975, *Keepers of the Gate: A History of Ellis Island*, New York: New York University Press, 15.

[17]Dr. Milton H. Foster, 1915, "A General Hospital for All Nations," Records of the Public Health Service, National Archives, RG 90.

[18]William Williams Papers, 1911, "A Brief History of Ellis Island," New York Public Library.

[19]Alfred C. Reed, 1912, "The Medical Side of Immigration," *Popular Science Monthly* LXXX: 384–390.

[20]Fitzhugh Mullan, 1989, *Plagues and Politics*, New York: Basic Books, 46–48.

[21]See Reed, "The Medical Side of Immigration," 384–390.

[22]Letter to the Acting Secretary of Commerce and Labor, March 13, 1911, from the Commissioner-General, Bureau of Immigration and Naturalization, General Immigration Files, National Archives, RG 90.

[23]Dr. Gertrude Slaughter, 1933, "America's Front Door," *Hygeia* XI (January), 11–14.

[24]Dr. Grover Kempf, Oral History interview conducted in 1977 and covering his Public Health Service experiences at Ellis Island in 1912.

[25]Ibid.

[26]Letter to Secretary of Commerce and Labor V. H. Metcalf, February 22, 1906, from President Theodore Roosevelt, General Immigration Files, National Archives, RG 90.

[27]Fiorello H. La Guardia, 1948, *The Making of an Insurgent*, New York: J. B. Lippincott, 62–75.

[28]See Fairchild, *Science at the Borders*, 42.

[29]Sally Loth, Oral History interview conducted in 1976 and covering her experiences as a social service worker on Ellis Island from 1914 to 1918.

[30]Letter to the Commissioner-General of Immigration, November 10, 1908, from Robert Watchorn, Commissioner of Immigration, Ellis Island, General Immigration Files, National Archives, RG 90.

CHAPTER 3

[1]Prof. Alan Kraut, 2000, videotaped interview at American University.

[2]John Gaquer, 1999, videotaped interview at the site of Ellis Island Hospital.

[3]Josephine Messina Cirella, Oral History interview conducted in 1992 and covering her immigration experience at Ellis Island in 1923.

[4]Dr. Bruce T. Anderson, Oral History interview conducted in 1977 and covering his experience as a Public Health physician in the Ellis Island Hospital in 1919.

[5]Dr. Milton H. Foster, 1915, "A General Hospital for All Nations," Records of the

Public Health Service, 1912–1968, General Immigration Files, RG 90.

[6]Josephine Lutomski, Oral History interview conducted in 1986 and covering her experience as a ward matron in the Ellis Island Hospital in 1922.

[7]Red Cross Narrative Report written by Elizabeth Gardiner, chief social service worker, Ellis Island Hospital, 1920, Ellis Island Library.

[8]Inge Matthies Nastke, Oral History interview conducted in 1986 and covering her experience as a patient at Ellis Island Hospital in 1922.

[9]Dr. John C. Thill, Oral History interview conducted in 1977 and covering his experience as a Public Health Service physician on Ellis Island in 1924.

[10]Dr. Bruce Anderson, Oral History interview conducted in 1977 and covering his experience as a Public Health Service physician on Ellis Island in 1919.

[11]Letter to Commissioner-General of Immigration, December 17, 1908, from Robert Watchorn, Ellis Island Commissioner of Immigration, General Immigration Files, National Archives, RG 90.

[12]Amy L. Fairchild, 2003, *Science at the Borders*. Baltimore, Md.: The Johns Hopkins University Press, 41.

[13]Howard Markel, fall 2000, "The Eyes Have It: Trachoma, the Perception of Disease, the United States Public Health Service, and the American Jewish Immigration Experience," 1897–1924, Bulletin of the History of Medicine 74, no. 3: 525–560.

[14]Josephine Gazieri Calloway, Oral History interview conducted in 1986 and covering her experience as a trachoma patient at the Ellis Island Hospital in 1922.

[15]Harlan Unrau, 1984, *Historic Resource Study*, vol. 2, New York: National Park Service, 724–730.

[16]Ibid.

[17]Ibid.

[18]Dr. Grover Kempf, Oral History interview conducted in 1977 and covering his Public Health Service experiences at Ellis Island in 1912.

[19]Dr. Eugene H. Mullan, 1913, "The Normal Immigrant," records of the Public Health Service, 1912–1968, General Immigration Files, RG 90.

[20]Henry Hall, November 20, 1913, "The Great American Hold-Up at Ellis Island," *The Sunday World*, records of the Public Health Service, General Immigration Files, National Archives, RG 90.

[21]Josephine Gazieri Calloway, Oral History interview conducted in 1986 and covering her experience as a trachoma patient at the Ellis Island Hospital in 1922.

[22]Florence A. Huxley, "ALA Work on Ellis Island," *Library Journal* XLV (April 15, 1920): 350–352, cited in Harlan Unrau, 1984, *Historic Resource Study*, vol. 11, National Park Service, 649.

[23]Edward Cholakian, Oral History interview conducted in 1990 and covering his experience as a trachoma patient at the Ellis Island Hospital in 1920.

[24]Red Cross Annual Report, 1915, Ellis Island Library.

[25]Red Cross Narrative Report, 1920, Ellis Island Library.

[26]Public Health Films, National Archives Motion Picture Division, College Park, Md.

[27]John Henry Wilberding, 2000, videotaped interview in Shepherd, Mich.

[28]Ibid.

[29]Barry Moreno, 2000, Ellis Island National Park librarian, videotaped interview.

[30]Dr. Bruce T. Anderson, Oral History interview conducted in 1977 and covering his experience as a Public Health Service physician at the Ellis Island Hospital in 1919.

[31]Anne McDermott Keeling, 2006, niece of Ormond McDermott, videotaped interview.

CHAPTER 4

[1]William Williams Papers, New York Public Library, 1912, "The Invasion of the Unfit," *Medical Record: A Weekly Journal of Medicine and Surgery*, December 14.

[2]William Williams Papers, New York Public Library, "Immigration and Insanity," from an address given by Williams before the Mental Hygiene Conference in New York City, November 14, 1912.

[3]Amy L. Fairchild, 2003, *Science at the Borders*, Baltimore, Md.: The Johns Hopkins University Press, 94: Alan Kraut, 1994, *Silent Travelers*, Baltimore, Md.: The Johns Hopkins University Press, 145.

[4]Letter to F. P. Sargent, Commissioner-General of Immigration, June 11, 1906, from Robert Watchorn, Ellis Island Commissioner of Immigration, General Immigration Files, National Archives, RG 85.

[5]Annual Report of the Surgeon General of the Public Health and Marine Hospital Service, 1905, cited in Harlan Unrau, *Historic Resource Study*, vol. 11, National Park Service: 596–597.

[6]William Williams Papers, New York Public Library.

[7]Ibid.

[8]Annual Report of the Surgeon General of the Public Health and Marine Hospital Service, 1905, cited in Unrau, *Historic Resource Study*, 596.

[9]Henry H. Goddard, "Feeblemindedness and Immigration," *Training School Bulletin* 9 (October 1912): 91–94.

[10]Annual Report of the Surgeon General of the Public Health and Marine Hospital Service, 1905, 271–278, cited in Unrau, *Historic Resource Study*, 598.

[11]See Kraut, *Silent Travelers*, 73–76.

[12]George McDaniel, "Madison Grant and the Racialist Movement," *American Renaissance*, www.amren.com/mtnews/archives/2005/09/madison_grant_a.php, accessed November 22, 2006.

[13]William Williams Papers, "Invasion of the Unfit," New York Public Library.

[14]Dr. J. G. Wilson, 1913, "A Study in Jewish Psychopathology," *Popular Science Monthly* 82: 265, 271.

[15]Dr. E. K. Sprague, 1914, "Mental Examination of Immigrants," *The Survey*, vol. 31, 466–468.

[16]Dr. L. L. Williams, 1914, "The Medical Inspection of Mentally Defective Aliens: Its Scope and Limitations," *American Journal of Insanity* 71: 269–277.

[17]"Comedies and Tragedies at Ellis Island," General Immigration Files, RG 85.

[18]Ibid.

[19]Dr. E. H. Mullan, cited in Amy L. Fairchild, *Science at the Borders*, 103.

[20]Dr. Grover Kempf, Oral History interview conducted in 1977 and covering his Public Health Service experiences at Ellis Island in 1912.

[21]Invoice from the *American Journal of Physical Anthropology* to the U.S. Public Health Service, May 1, 1926: "1 set of anthropometric instruments, consisting of 3 metal calipers, to be used in measuring immigrants . . . $60.00 . . ." General Immigration Files, National Archives, RG 90.

[22]Letter from Arles Hrdlicka, curator of physical anthropology at the Smithsonian Institution, to Surgeon General Rupert Blue, January 21, 1919, General Immigration Files, RG 85.

[23]Letter from Arles Hrdlicka, curator of physical anthropology at the Smithsonian Institution, to Surgeon General H. S. Cumming, March 6, 1926, General Immigration Files, RG 85.

[24]See Kraut, *Silent Travelers*, 75.

[25]Fiorello H. La Guardia, 1948, *The Making of an Insurgent*, New York: J. B. Lippincott, 65.

[26]Linnea Hallgren, 1999, videotaped interview at the subject's home in Cape Cod, Mass.

CHAPTER 5

[1]Letter from Frederick A. Wallis, U.S. Commissioner of Immigration at Ellis Island, to Secretary of Labor James J. Davis, 1921, General Records of the Department of Labor, National Archives, RG 174.

[2]Alfred C. Reed, 1913, "Going Through Ellis Island," *Popular Science Monthly* LXXXII, 13.

[3]Harlan Unrau, 1984, *Historic Resource Study*, vol. 11, National Park Service, 629.

[4]Molly Billings, http://www.theinfluenza pandemicof1918@virus.stanford.edu/uda/.

[5]Report to the Secretary of the Treasury, written by Eliot Wadsworth, assistant secretary of the treasury, September 21, 1923, General Immigration Files, RG 90.

[6]Annual Report of the Surgeon General of the Public Health Service, 1921, General Immigration Files, RG 90.

[7]See Unrau, *Historic Resource Study*, vol. II, 629.

[8]Cited in Henry Guzda, 1986, "Keeper of the Gate: Ellis Island a Welcome Site? Only After Years of Reform," *Monthly Labor Review* (July), 35.

[9]Titanic Nautical Society and Resource Center, "Immigration Laws in 1912—Titanic," www. titanic-nautical.com/RMS-Titanic-Immigration-

Laws-1912.html, accessed September 4, 2006.

[10]Philip Kunhardt, Jr., et. al., 1999, *Preacher of Prosperity*, New York: Riverhead Books, 272–281.

[11]"A Short History of U.S. Immigration Policy, the 1920s and 1930s: A 'Pause' or an Ugly Period in American History?" American Immigration Law Foundation, www.ailf.org/ipc/policy_reports_1996_pr9613.htm#2, accessed November 2006.

[12]*The New York Times*, December 20, 1924.

[13]Prof. Alan Kraut, videotaped interview, 2006, New York City, and Dr. Howard Markel, videotaped interview, 2006, Cambridge, Mass. Also see Howard Markel, 1997, *Quarantine! East European Jewish Immigrants and the New York City Epidemics of 1892*, Baltimore, Md.: The Johns Hopkins University Press, 183–193; and Alan Kraut, 1994, *Silent Travelers*, Baltimore, Md.: The Johns Hopkins University Press, 108–111.

[14]Dr. John Thill, Oral History interview conducted in 1977 and covering his experience as a Public Health Service physician on Ellis Island in 1924.

[15]See Unrau, *Historic Resource Study*, vol. III, 896.

INDEX